# Real Life Diaries

## LIVING WITH
## MENTAL ILLNESS

True stories by ordinary people about facing challenges, living with stigma, and finding hope in life with mental illness

LYNDA CHELDELIN FELL

with

CARRIE WORTHINGTON

A portion of proceeds from the sale of this book is donated to National Alliance for Mental Illness, a not-for-profit organization dedicated to building better lives for the millions affected by mental illness. For more information, visit www.nami.org.

AlyBlue
MEDIA

Real Life Diaries
Living with Mental Illness – 1st ed.
True stories by ordinary people about facing challenges, living with stigma, and finding hope in life with mental illness
Lynda Cheldelin Fell/Carrie Worthington
Real Life Diaries www.RealLifeDiaries.com

Cover Design by AlyBlue Media, LLC
Interior Design by AlyBlue Media LLC
Published by AlyBlue Media, LLC

ISBN: 978-1-944328-50-4
Library of Congress Control Number: 2017945931
AlyBlue Media, LLC
Ferndale, WA 98248
www.AlyBlueMedia.com

PRINTED IN THE UNITED STATES OF AMERICA

AlyBlue
MEDIA

Living with Mental Illness

# DEDICATION

This book is dedicated to all
who live with mental illness

# CONTENTS

BY KARIN RING

# INTRODUCTION

We sit across from each other in fervent silence. Our resolve? To look at our nails (should have trimmed those down), our shoes (I really need to clean this pair), or the current issue of People magazine about Tom and Katie. Every once in a while we look up to smile briefly at the new face that comes in for an appointment.

But yet in all of our resolve, we are a person, a representative of what our vast different worlds have in common. We are the mentally ill. Bipolar, manic depressive, psychotic, schizophrenia, addiction, personality disorders, fears, repression, just to name only a tenth of a few. As we live and cope with our daily life of imbalance, we strain hard to keep up in an unforgiving world of mental disorders. We go silently to doctors, AA, group therapies, and counseling to give us a hopeful light not at the end, but at the beginning of our journey.

As we dedicate ourselves to healing and improvement, we see ourselves as the world's future. We are your future doctors, nurses, lawyers, president, franchise owner, entrepreneur. Yes, we may be the mentally ill for now, but we will overcome. We have overcome.

As we look at each other and smile in that waiting room contemplating nails, shoes, Tom and Katie, we understand each other.

And we know that from here on out, we are the mentally healed. *For God has not given us a spirit of fear, but of power and of love and of a sound mind* (2 Timothy 1:7). Amen

-KAREN RING

BY LYNDA CHELDELIN FELL

# PREFACE

Mental illness—two words that strike fear in society. As a child, I heard stories about my maternal great-grandmother who suffered from melancholy so severe, it left her bedridden. I always wondered what life was like for her. Did she lay in bed crying? Did she ever find moments of hope? Back then it was believed that depression was all in one's head but if medication had been available, would my great-grandmother have been able to lead a life worth living? She died before I was born, so I never had the chance to find out.

Years later I was stricken with my first major depressive episode and learned firsthand the deep sadness and hopelessness felt by my great-grandmother. For me, depression was like being caught in a dark hole with no energy to climb out. It was as if someone had robbed my world of Technicolor, and life was now cloaked in shades of gray. But I had one major life-saving advantage that wasn't available to my great-grandmother: medication.

Prozac entered my life, and sound, color and beauty returned to my world. I was no longer going through the motions cloaked by a heavy wet blanket. Life felt worth living again. Highly effective and nonaddictive, Prozac became quite popular, almost fashionable, and within a few short years had been dispensed to millions. And yet the societal stigma against mental illness remained steadfast.

According to the National Alliance on Mental Illness, over 40 million people experience some form of mental illness each year; it's nondiscriminatory, and can affect anyone.

When faced with a stigmatized journey where understanding and compassion remain scarce, it's important that we work together to remove the stigma so those affected by mental illness don't hide like my great-grandmother did. In today's world, people can find the support and treatment they need to lead a rich, fulfilling life. Let's not let stigma stop them from doing that.

Helen Keller said, "Walking with a friend in the dark is better than walking alone in the light." If you are one of millions who live with mental illness or love someone who does, the following true stories are written by courageous people who share your path. Although no two journeys are identical, we hope you'll find comfort in these stories and the understanding that you aren't truly alone. For we walk ahead, behind, and right beside you.

Warm regards,

*Lynda Cheldelin Fell*

CREATOR, REAL LIFE DIARIES
www.LyndaFell.com

# CHAPTER ONE

# Starting Out

Begin today. Declare out loud to the universe that you are willing to let go of struggle and eager to learn through joy. -SARAH BAN BREATHNACH

Being diagnosed with a mental illness can be a long, drawn-out process. Without the benefit of lab testing, establishing a proper diagnosis can take a while, sometimes even long after we're aware something is wrong. When the diagnosis is reached at last, some feel relief for finally having an explanation for our thoughts and behavior. Others feel shame, anger, and confusion because of the stereotypes and prejudices about mental illness. To fully appreciate the unique perspectives, it's helpful to understand the different journeys. In this chapter, each writer shares the beginning of her story.

*

ADRIANNE ALLEN-LANG
Adrianne was diagnosed with dissociative
identity disorder in 2015 at age 18

My parents split when I was two and a half years old. The night before my mother left is my earliest memory, and is the night when I birthed my dissociative identity disorder. I remember walking out to speak with my parents, and asking them to stop yelling because I was trying to sleep. My mother put me back to bed, and when I woke up again she was gone.

For the next ten years, I bounced between my parents who couldn't be within meters of each other. I have many memories of them screaming at one another outside the car during custody exchanges. It was so bad that my father would not come to any of my school award ceremonies, all because my mother would be there and he'd start a scene.

My father was never involved with us very much, and would buy us expensive things so we wouldn't bother him. He moved to the city with us when I was nine. Prior to that, we would go back down to the country town and spend every second weekend with him and his friend. When I was four, his friend started molesting me, and I was too scared to say anything. Kitty was birthed to deal with the trauma.

My father also groomed me from a young age to prepare to leave my mum. He would always drill into my head that she hated my brother and me, and that we needed to be with him to be safe.

When I was twelve, I moved from living with my mother full-time to living with my father, his girlfriend, and her three kids. At this time, I was in grade six of primary school and was getting bullied savagely. I was suicidal and using my dissociation and alters to get through each day. At this stage, there were four of us including Az (host), Pumpkin (core), Kitty, and Adrian. My father's girlfriend at the time, M, and her kids would beat me. If I ever fought back to the kids, M would beat me even more and force me to do everyone's chores while her kids got to lounge around and throw things at me.

When I was thirteen the bullying escalated and I was given the typical responses, "What did you do to provoke them?"

"Just move away."

"That doesn't sound like the truth."

"Your fault for having your bra showing."

My first year of high school birthed my fifth alter, Anna, a mute that I used to survive the bullying. I was thrown off moving buses, had my things stolen and thrown in trees, and faced a barrage of verbal and physical abuse as well. The second year of high school birthed number six, named Keegan. He started a lot of problems including fighting, violence, drugs, and alcohol.

One afternoon during class, a child was hitting me in the back. After warning him three times to stop, we just snapped and belted the life out of him. We had to be pulled off by two male students, and that was the end of that school. After being removed from there, I suffered a psychotic breakdown where I had to be sectioned (detained under the Mental Health Act) for a week due to being a threat to myself and apparently others. I was held down, had my piercings ripped out of my ears, and was handcuffed to a hospital bed and ambulance gurney, all because I wanted to be left alone.

My diary was found telling about my self-harming, suicide, and others in my head, but it was used against me. I was thirteen at this time. This started a downward spiral of impulsive, reckless relationships, underage prostitution, and drug abuse, which didn't ease up until my second pregnancy. During this stage, I became pregnant with my first son due to a drug-hazed rape. I was belted within an inch of my life during school when I was seventeen weeks pregnant, and miscarried due to it. My alter Allie came about from this, the motherly feminist.

I went home to my father. His girlfriend pinned me up against a wall by my throat, told me I was a disgrace, useless, and to leave and never come back, or she would kill me. I went back to my mother for a bit but the local abuse escalated and I couldn't cope, so I fled across the country, where I met my son's father. He was highly physically, mentally, emotionally and financially abusive to me, as well as being a hardcore drug addict. I was too scared to leave, and at twelve weeks pregnant with my son, after a hospital stay and nearly losing him, I came home to abuse again. My son's father spent eight hundred dollars on drugs and then started on me. He punched a hole through a wall and left me screaming in a corner, crying out that I'd rather kill myself and our baby than spend another second with him.

Suddenly it felt like I was in a haze as I left him. I hated what I was doing, but I couldn't stop, even as he was laying into me. I just kept moving around and packing up, protecting my stomach. I have since found out that it was an alter who ultimately saved my life and my child's. Without my head mates, I believe we'd be dead either at the hands of my son's father, or by our own. I have an introject (an internal projected image of an abuser) of my son's father; his name is Muscle. Muscle torments me with nightmares and traumatic flashbacks, which means I don't sleep much.

Since becoming a mother at sixteen, there have been more experiences of abuse that have not birthed new alters, but brought pre-existing ones to the surface. It is a constant learning experience, especially when new rooms or things pop up in my inner world. There are currently ten of us, including Az, Adrianne, Kitty, Pumpkin,

Keegan, Muscle, Nurse, Harley, Myrnin and Anna. I have no doubt you'll hear from them throughout this book.

*

MORGAN BUTLER
Morgan was diagnosed with depression
and anxiety in 2009 at age 15

You might say that I was predisposed for this kind of diagnosis. There are so many factors that can lead to mental illness: the biological, the environmental—the cards seemed stacked against me. On my maternal side, most of the women have disorders, namely bipolar, or manic depression as it's sometimes referred to as. My mother suffered from this along with addiction, and fell victim to her vices while pregnant with me. I was born healthy by all accounts, but these predispositions and my mother's habits led to environmental issues in my upbringing. Being split between households and witnessing a variety of inconsistencies in my early life, I soon began showing signs of separation anxiety and other behavioral red flags.

You see, I was a good kid, generally. I was independent, listened to my teachers, everything you'd expect of a student. My report cards said I was shy but smart and sweet. But there were also the breakdowns. Sometimes I'd crawl under my desk and just cry, taking refuge from the world.

In my preteen and early teenage years, I began wearing baggy clothing, avoided most girly clothes, and hung around a crowd of more alternative persons. I still pushed for good grades, but I paid less attention in class. I participated in extracurriculars, but I listened to darker music and began to write poetry and keep a journal of the darkness that I was experiencing inside.

I then began cutting. At first it was simple—a small coping mechanism where I'd just scrape at my skin, or use an eraser to create a sort of rug burn. This is when I realized that my problem was deeper than just "emo" feelings, as the current pop culture put it. The problem worsened, and my methods became more destructive. The official diagnosis came in 2009, when I was a stupid, young teenage girl who was interested in a high school senior. My parents found out and forbid a relationship. I ended up going behind their back, which led to my transfer of high schools. Dismayed, I attempted suicide.

My stepmom found my diary a few months later and immediately took me to our doctor. He saw my arms, gave me a survey to fill out, and then referred me to a psychiatrist who diagnosed depression and anxiety. I refused medication and barely succumbed to the prescribed counseling sessions each week. I went for six months and then told my parents I had everything in check.

Don't get me wrong, I believe psychological help is extremely important. It's crucial to recognize you have an issue and to seek help. I believe there needs to be more compassion in the world and openness for mental illness. It isn't taboo, and we need to be willing to help one another; to not be embarrassed of our scars or ashamed of our vulnerability.

I believe that everyone with mental illness is different. Some need medication, some need cognitive behavioral therapy to learn coping mechanisms and how to keep themselves in check, some need long-term counseling. It's all okay, and one treatment isn't better or worse. It all depends on the individual.

In 2012, I experienced one of the worst times of my life to this day: I lost a close friend to suicide. On April 10, 2012, Alex, a girl my age on a similar path to mine, took her own life. This was a very trying experience for those of us in our circle of friends. At the pinnacle of our high school career, just months before graduation, I had essentially lost a sister. In the following weeks, I realized just how much this impacted my life, and the lives of others. It made me think about what could have happened if I had been successful in my own past attempts. I remembered how much my stepmom cried when she found out that I was self-mutilating. She thought she was doing something wrong, and even fell into a year of her own kind of depression and self-blame.

I realized that even though our mental health is internal, there are so many external impacts. Therefore, I must be conscientious of the wonderful people in my life and how there are true reasons to keep going, even when depression gives you this illusion that life lacks meaning or purpose. Depression is deceptive and it is so wrong about you. Sometimes it takes hard measures to realize that.

*

LYNDA CHELDELIN FELL
Lynda was diagnosed with depression in 2000 at age 35
and posttraumatic stress disorder in 2012 at age 47

Depression runs in my family, as does prejudice against mental illness. I was raised in an era where one didn't admit flaws for fear of tarnishing the family name. This isn't anything against my parents; it's just how many in their generation feel about sharing something as intimate as mental illness. It was seen as airing dirty laundry of sorts.

My first bout of depression occurred years before my first official diagnosis, which came in my thirties following a nonnegotiable hysterectomy. I was experiencing heavily vaginal bleeding from two uterine fibroid tumors. The blood loss led to severe anemia, and surgery was my only option. The size of the fibroids meant a total abdominal hysterectomy. I had no other option.

I was the fourth child out of five and enjoyed being part of a large, loving family. Although we already had four kids, I wanted a fifth. I loved being a mother, and despite the morning sickness, I loved everything about pregnancy, birthing, and motherhood. To this day, I still consider motherhood a treasured gift.

When I was diagnosed with two large fibroid tumors and severe anemia, my gynecologist immediately booked me for a total abdominal hysterectomy. At the time, I thought I was okay with it. After all, I didn't have any other option. I tried telling myself that at least I got to skip all the perimenopause stuff I watched my own mother suffer through. But it didn't help. Before I knew it I was mourning the loss of my womb, but I couldn't share it with anyone for fear they might think I was being ridiculous.

Over time, I noticed that life felt hopeless. Without my womb, I felt un-womanly. Such emotions are commonly associated with a mastectomy because the absence of breasts are more obvious than the absence of a cervix and uterus. But inside I felt lesser than, like half a woman. The color began draining from my life, replaced by varying shades of gray which soon grew to black. I had no idea I was sinking into major depression, I just knew life felt hopeless.

The best way I can describe it is a feeling of being caught in a deep, dark hole. Even if someone had leaned into the hole with an outstretched hand, I didn't have the energy to reach up and grab it. It was that bad.

Truth be told, there was absolutely nothing wrong in my life. I had a good marriage and four wonderful kids whom I adored. We had a lovely home, pets, and our kids were active in a variety of sports. My extended family was all doing well, and I had absolutely no explanation for feeling . . . so heavy . . . so lost . . . so . . . nothing.

By the time I sought help, I didn't care whether I lived or died. I didn't have an active suicide plan, but it didn't matter. Life felt hopeless, so if I were hit by a bus, it would have been welcomed.

When I finally sought help, the doctor immediately diagnosed me with major depression. I was put on Prozac, which carried as much stigma as my new diagnosis. But I had nothing to lose and everything to gain. So I accepted the prescription. And it worked. Thus began an on-again, off-again relationship with Prozac.

I had known for years that my maternal great-grandmother suffered greatly with depression. Without the benefit of medication back in those days, she was completely bedridden. My heart broke for the life she led, knowing it could have been me.

Fast forward to 2009, and life threw us a terrible curveball: our fifteen-year-old daughter was killed in a car accident while coming home from a swim meet. Knowing my susceptibility for major depression, my doctor immediately restarted my Prozac. It didn't quell the grief, but it did prevent me from sinking into that horrible black hole. Was I suicidal? Yes. But the suicidal ideation stemmed from losing my daughter, not from depression.

The posttraumatic stress disorder diagnosis came later. On the night of the accident, I sat with my daughter's body in the field next to the crushed cars. Less than three years later, I witnessed my forty-six-year-old husband having a major stroke that robbed him completely of speech, reading, writing and math capabilities, and left him paralyzed on one side. At some point in the aftermath, I was diagnosed with posttraumatic stress disorder. Strangely enough, nobody ever handed me that diagnosis. I saw it listed in my medical records. When I researched PTSD, I discovered that I did indeed have many of the symptoms. But why did my doctor never tell me? Having an explanation for my symptoms would have been most welcome.

*

SHELBY COLICH JOHNSON
Shelby was diagnosed with
depression in 2005 at age 12

It's difficult to remember what life was like before depression came into the picture, because that's what it is—a life before and a life after. Before the diagnosis, I had a short fuse or would spend hours crying alone. I didn't feel happy the way the rest of the world appeared to be happy. Things I once enjoyed doing, like drawing, softball, and spending time with my friends, were no longer a priority for me. I actually preferred spending time alone because I didn't want to chance people I loved having to deal with my mood swings. I loved them, and I knew they loved me, but they wouldn't understand. How could they understand when I didn't even know how to explain it to myself? From the moment I woke up every morning until I cried myself to sleep at night, I felt alone and hopeless.

After a few years, it became clear that this wasn't just a case of average teenage hormones. My mom set up an appointment with a psychiatrist and at fourteen-years-old, I was officially diagnosed with major depression. The various antidepressants and therapists helped for a while, but I still wasn't happy. I felt like I was just going through the motions on autopilot.

It wasn't until I got my first job the summer before my senior year of high school that I finally sensed some of that black cloud, which had lingered over my life for the better part of a decade, begin to diminish. I started making new friends who didn't know of my illness. If I wasn't at school or at work, I was spending the remainder of my time with my new friends and my first serious boyfriend. It's not that my depression just magically went away—it was always with me, lying dormant as long as I was keeping myself as busy as I possibly could. But the moment I would stop to think, there it was waiting for me.

My boyfriend, Zach, helped me realize a person can do more than just exist with depression, he showed me how to live with it. Zach had been dealing with clinical depression by himself since about the same time I was first diagnosed. I started focusing all of my spare time on helping Zach because it helped me too. It helped me to focus on someone else's needs for a change, it helped us better understand our illnesses. It helped to know in a world where we spent so many years believing we were alone, we'd always have each other.

*

SHAUNA COX
Shauna was diagnosed with an
anxiety disorder in 2009 at age 26

I was twenty-six years old when I was officially given the diagnosis of having an anxiety disorder. When the psychologist first gave me this diagnosis, I remember feeling a sense of relief. I was relieved to finally have a real reason for why I was feeling the way I was, and I felt hope that there was a treatment for this disorder; it wasn't just who I was as a person, but something that could be tackled and won.

Initially, I was also a little embarrassed but not because of the diagnosis. I was embarrassed to be going through the symptoms I was experiencing. One of the features of my anxiety disorder is panic, but not the type that most people have heard about. I had learned about panic disorder in university, but I was taught the symptoms of a racing heart, trouble breathing, and feeling like you are about to die. My panic symptoms, on the other hand, mainly involved feeling hot, sometimes sweating, and having diarrhea. I was so afraid of being in line anywhere (the grocery store and the airport being big triggers), and not being able to "escape" to go to the bathroom. This would then often trigger the panic symptoms I was so afraid of. As soon as I was out of the anxiety-triggering situation, the panic would slowly start to go away and I would relax.

Shortly after receiving my diagnosis, and while I was just beginning medication and therapy, my husband and I were planning our wedding. As you can probably imagine, standing up in front of people for our wedding was an anxiety-provoking-no-escape situation. I kept imagining being in my white dress in front of friends and family, and needing to race to the bathroom. What would be worse than the bride suddenly racing away from the altar? The bride not making it away from the altar in time in a white dress. So, my strategy was two-fold: take the maximum dose of my anxiolytic medication that my doctor had prescribed, and have a second wedding dress in case of my worst-case accident scenario. While I didn't need my second wedding dress, I wish that I had progressed further in therapy with my psychologist before getting married. What I didn't realize is that the anxiolytic can cause memory blackouts, and I am sad that there are big chunks of my wedding day that I don't remember.

Still, I finally had a real, concrete answer as to why I was feeling the way that I was feeling, and I could see a light at the end of my anxious tunnel. Now that I have strategies to handle the anxiety, and I have made significant progress in fighting the disorder, I am a lot more open about the diagnosis, and any embarrassment I initially felt has disappeared.

*

JANE MCDONALD
Jane was diagnosed with major depressive disorder in 1989,
multiple anxiety disorders in 2001, multiple personality
disorders in 2007, and dissociative identity disorder in 2014

I cannot recall a time when I was not struggling with some form of mental illness. The truth is I don't have much memory of my early years other than feeling profoundly sad most of the time. My parents had separated and fought constantly. I lived with my mother and sister, who could both be very hurtful and negative. Emotions were not to be expressed in my household, particularly negative emotions such as sadness, anxiety, or anger. As a result, I told no one when I started feeling deeply depressed much of the time or when I would worry so much about school or my father, who also struggled with mental illness. I learned to keep it all bottled up inside, which is now one of the worst things they say you can do. But at the time, that was the only way I could survive. Things only got worse for me. I fought constantly with my sister and was bullied extensively at school from the age of ten onward. It was at this point that my depression became too much for me to bear, and after expressing my profound unhappiness in a writing assignment at school, I was taken to see the

13

school guidance counselor. He then referred me to my family doctor who made the official diagnosis of depression. This was around age ten and although I saw my doctor weekly to talk about what was going on in my life, very little changed. In fact, things only continued to get worse.

Around this same time, I was also being sexually abused by two different people. One was a close family member and, thus, I feared speaking out against him because I thought I would not be believed. The other individual was the son of a couple who were close friends with my parents. Although the abuse never became physical, the constant verbal abuse and sexual assaults served to worsen my depression and lead to feelings of extreme shame and anxiety. It felt like nowhere was safe for me. I was unhappy at home, at school, with family, etc... I was extremely socially withdrawn and highly anxious of any social situation.

My depression and anxiety continued to get worse throughout my years in high school and I became acutely suicidal. I began to self-harm as a method of coping with my strong emotions and was hospitalized at one point for a week in an attempt to treat the suicidal ideation and depression. The week did nothing for me except make me learn to keep my emotions and my cutting even more of a secret. After being released I was forced to start regular therapy with a counselor, as well as group therapy. These were ineffective at best. My mental health continued to deteriorate as I progressed through, and graduated, high school and then went away.

By the time I was in university, I was acutely suicidal and suffered from severe anxiety as well as depression. I was officially diagnosed with social anxiety disorder, general anxiety disorder, panic disorder,

PTSD, and several phobias (as well as major depressive disorder) in 2001. Although some might be overwhelmed by the sheer number of diagnoses, none of this came as a particular surprise as I had been living with these symptoms for years. I was also studying college psychology and was well aware that what I was experiencing was not normal and were, in fact, signs of major mental illnesses. Again, I sought out help first at the counseling center on campus and was then referred to an outside therapist, neither of which were particularly helpful. I was placed on antidepressants and antianxiety medications which took the edge off my symptoms, but were not a complete solution. I was still chronically depressed, highly anxious, and still chronically struggled with self-harm and suicidal ideation. During my time at university, I was also hospitalized a number of times in the psych ward, but this only made things worse. It also made it difficult for me to maintain a minimum course load. As a result of mental illnesses, it took me a significantly longer amount of time for me to complete the program. I did eventually succeed, and graduated with an Honors B.A.

Following university, I entered yet another abusive relationship. I finally had enough and fled both the relationship and the city I was living in. I wanted to put as much distance as possible between me and my ex. Once in my new city and with a new doctor, I was referred to a psychologist at the local psychiatric hospital who was part of the personality disorders program: borderline personality disorder, dependent personality disorder, and avoidant personality disorder. The borderline diagnosis had been suggested to me by a professor during my university years but had never officially been diagnosed. As I read up on my new diagnosis it all started to make much more sense. A few years later (due to a long waiting list), I entered an intensive outpatient treatment program for people who have personality disorders. Unfortunately, this program, much like all therapies I had received in the past, proved to be of limited success.

After completing the intensive outpatient program, I was referred to my current psychiatrist, who gave me my latest diagnosis of dissociative identity disorder. This diagnosis did take me a bit by surprise but, again, in reading up on the signs and symptoms it fit with what I had been experiencing since childhood. This diagnosis had actually been documented in my file years earlier but the doctors never mentioned it to me. Having an explanation for the symptoms I'd been experiencing would've been extremely helpful and reassuring, so this last diagnosis was met with surprise and more than a little frustration.

I am currently on a number of psychiatric medications and am in bi-weekly therapy. I find my symptoms tend to go in cycles and are better at some times, but then flare up. It is a daily struggle living with so many different mental illnesses but it is a fight worth fighting.

*

AMY OWEN
Amy was diagnosed with ADD and
bipolar disorder in 2014 at age 42

As a child, I had a very hard time in school. I could not concentrate and was very hyper. My parents had me tested before they knew what attention deficit disorder was. The school wanted to put me in a special classroom and not deal with me. My parents refused. Not having anyone who understood what I was going through, I just scraped by. I went to college and did pretty well. I found that smoking pot helped me focus more and calm me down. I loved the feeling. For the first time, my brain was not going ninety miles an hour.

All my life I wanted to be a mom. After a year of trying and much disappointment, my husband and I went through in vitro fertilization. This was in the late 1990s, so they were still figuring out the best way to do it. The first round did not work and it brought on my first bout of depression. Not taking time to recover, I went through IVF again and got pregnant with twins.

They were very healthy babies. I became very nervous and scared, being responsible for these beautiful babies. This was the start of my panic attacks. I was put on antidepressants and antianxiety medicine. They seemed to help. Wanting another child, I slowly went off and got pregnant with my third child naturally. She was very healthy and I went back on the meds after she was born.

I was also given pain meds and found I had more confidence and was much happier taking them. I had very bad migraines and a young doctor gave me large amounts of pain meds whenever I asked, and I became addicted. After about a year, I went into rehab. It helped for a little while, but I went back to taking them. I could no longer get them on a regular basis, so I became very depressed and anxious.

Going up and down and not taking anything for depression, I spiraled into a very manic state and made some really bad decisions. I took the kids and left my husband and close family to move to Texas with extended family I trusted would help. I stopped taking the pain meds and was diagnosed with ADD. This helped so much. I had a clear head but was still very manic. The family I had in Texas were not good influences, and they took advantage of my situation. I got divorced and became very angry with my parents and my brother and his wife. Knowing I had no one to turn to, my cousin kicked me out of the house I rented from her.

I wanted to stay in Texas and prove I could make it on my own, so instead of reaching for my ex-husband, who was very angry at me, I reached out to a man ten years younger. He used to be addicted to pain medication and I thought we could help each other. Instead, he introduced me to a stronger pain med. He became very controlling and abusive to me but wanted my kids to like him, so he did it when they were with their dad. I didn't want the kids to see this, so they spent more and more time away. This sent me into a deep depression.

After eight months, I couldn't take it anymore. I called my parents and they came to get me and the kids. I lost everything. We came back to Illinois with only two weeks of clothes and nothing else. The kids were very angry because I took them away from their dad a second time. I went to the doctor and she diagnosed me with depression, anxiety and ADD. This helped for a while. My first husband came back and lived with me and the kids in my parent's house. Living with three people who were very angry with me, and a mom who was very controlling and an alcoholic, I became manic again. I slept around and tried to keep a man who was an alcoholic. I started a full-time job in an office, but I was so unhappy and stressed I had a very bad panic attack. On good advice from two people I worked with, I went into the hospital and found a really good doctor. She did not diagnose me with bipolar disorder right away, but after my hospital stay and seeing me in the aftercare program, she changed her mind and put me on antidepressants, mood stabilizers and ADD meds. Taking these as instructed has changed my life. I feel normal and can make good decisions. I have a good job and I am a great mom. I am working with my ex-husband so we can be together for our kids.

\*

AMBER PILLARS
Amber was diagnosed with
schizophrenia in 2004 at age 24

Spring 2004: I was offered my big job just out of college. This should've been the happiest time of my life, but it wasn't. I met my friend, Craig, while working at a camp in the summer of 2003. I was offered a youth job at the same time that Craig shared his heart with me.

"Amber, I'm moving closer to my family this fall to finish my master's degree. I'm ready to get married and start a family. I'm financially stable. I'm just looking for the girl to go with me. Oh, by the way, I've only told you and Jasmine (his recent ex-girlfriend)."

This wasn't exactly a proposal, but I wanted to follow him to another state more than anything in this world. I didn't tell my family about Craig and I's conversation. I thought they wouldn't be thrilled about me following a guy to another state without an engagement ring. Without telling anyone why, I got an extension on my decision for the youth job. I managed to miraculously get two job interviews within the week in that state.

But as fate would have it, both jobs were a bust. I couldn't count on either one of them. I sobbed the day I made my decision to stay in Iowa. I sobbed more when I told Craig.

We were both hurting deeply, but he attempted to put on a smile. He offered to help me find a plant for my new place. A couple of weeks later, I went to visit him. I guess it got too hard because Craig never did help me pick out a plant. But I still hoped and prayed that if we were meant to be together, we would work it out somehow.

Fall 2004: I was trying to focus on my new job. Truthfully, I was becoming more depressed about my situation. My heart was still with him; I felt dead inside without him. To this day, Craig has never moved out of state to be closer to his family.

I continued to struggle, thinking I was tough and could handle this myself. I had made it through some really rough situations in high school, I could do it again. My undiagnosed depression stemmed from a combination of events in high school and current stressful situations. My deeply rooted pain overwhelmed me.

December 2004: I was frightened my coworker wanted me fired. One week, I barely ate and slept. I called my parents from my closet. I was scared. That weekend, my mom took me to the primary care doctor in my hometown. At this point, I realized I needed help. I hardly took medicine. I was a lightweight and non-drowsy cold medicine knocked me out. After meeting with the doctor, I chose to take an antidepressant because I was willing to try to get better.

As the week passed by, I grew more and more frightened that my life was one big conspiracy and people were trying to kill me. Eventually, I chose to be admitted into the psychiatric unit of the hospital. I thought I would be safe there. The nurse told me it would only be a couple of days. During that stay, I began to hear people talking to me, but they weren't in the room with me. I didn't hear it with my ears but it was more of thoughts coming from the temples of my head. The voices were harsh and verbally abusive, telling me I was gross and ugly. Soon, I thought that I was pregnant. I knew I had not slept with any man. Therefore, I believed my baby was the second coming of Christ. When I told a nurse, she told me that it was my illness. I didn't know what she was talking about because I was only depressed.

Christmas was a couple of days away. I was angry. I was still in the hospital. Since I came voluntarily, I demanded to be able to leave to see my family for Christmas. I did get to leave, only I was leaving against medical advice.

My family had always brought a smile to my face, but my mind continued to betray me. At the extended family Christmas party, I watched a movie with my girl cousins. I was now convinced that movie was about me and people were plotting to kill me. I was terrified!

January 2005: I was sure Craig had asked my dad if he could marry me, though I hadn't heard from him since my last week of work. My parents always host the extended family Christmas party. My dad knew I needed a quiet place, so he took me to my brother's place. When I woke up, I was convinced my sister-in-law was hiding Craig. We were supposed to be together. The world was ending, and Craig was the missing link to saving the world. When we got back to the Christmas party, I yelled at my sister-in-law. "If you don't return Craig to me, you are going to pay." I never was going to hurt her, but God was the one she would have to answer to.

After that, I prayed the rosary every night with my parents. One night, my oldest brother came over. He told me I was going to the hospital. I became angry; I hated the hospital! Then next morning, I agreed to go to the hospital, but only because I was given an ultimatum. Either I could go with my parents, or with the cops. I chose to ride with my parents.

A short time passed and I was given a lawyer. I wasn't exactly sure what was happening. I tried to explain to the lawyer about the conspiracy against me and the end of the world, but I guess it never came out of my mouth that way. I soon realized that I was being committed in the psychiatric unit. They were making me take antipsychotic medicine. Since I refused the medicine orally, the nurses began injecting me. I remember the medicine knocked me out within minutes of getting the injection. Several times, big male nurses or cops would hold me down, therefore I learned to stop fighting the injections.

My parents, family members, and my best friend would come visit me during every visiting hour. I was convinced that Craig was in the psychiatric unit with me, only Craig had somehow morphed into this much older guy. The delusions were so strong that I began spending time with this much older guy. The nurses kept trying to keep me away from "Craig," which made me only want to be near him more. During this time, nurses tried to get me to sign some papers but I kept refusing. I was NOT signing anything! One day, my dad and oldest brother came to visit me and asked me to sign the papers. I am not sure what made me trust my family in that moment, but I signed it. I found out later that a ton of people were praying for me in the exact moment I signed the papers. Signing those papers saved my life.

February 2005: I was released to a different hospital. I was only there a short time when I became scared because all my muscles became so tight that I couldn't move and they were stuck in unnatural ways. I saw on TV that Pope John Paul II was dying. I became scared I was dying. So I finally told the nurses and my parents that I would take whatever I needed to get better. I allowed them to give me medicine immediately. I was out within seconds.

I started to improve a little. I thought when I moved to this new hospital, Craig had morphed into this smaller guy more my age. The nurses kept trying to stop us from kissing, but we kept finding ways to be close to each other. I am normally not that type of girl, but in my mind, it was Craig, whom I was going to marry.

Even still, I was improving enough to be released from the hospital. That's when my mom gave me a letter sent in the mail from Craig. I had to have been getting better, because I was confused as to why I had a letter from Craig, when the guy in the hospital had given me his address and phone number too.

I went home with my parents for the long, long journey to recovery. Eventually, I began to realize that all those things I thought were actually delusions, hallucinations, and me hearing voices. The psychiatrist diagnosed me with schizophrenia. With the help of God, psychiatrists, counselors, medicine, family and friends, I was able to recover. I live a productive and independent life again.

\*

DENISE PURCELL
Denise was diagnosed with depression, posttraumatic stress disorder, and dissociative identity disorder in 1995 at age 30

I had always felt down for no apparent reason. Some days, I wouldn't have even gotten out of bed if it weren't for my girls to take care of. I had two older daughters and three younger daughters. Two were twins.

I had a few failed marriages. One was abusive in every aspect. I came from a dysfunctional family. There were too many kids and there was not enough money or attention to go around. That was back in the days of "Don't cry or I'll give you something to cry about." Kids should be seen and not heard, but in my case it was safer to be both, not seen or heard.

I grew up alone and lonely. There was also sexual abuse, incest in the family, but we weren't supposed to tell anyone what went on in our house, so things were pushed aside and never dealt with.

I always heard voices that were more like statements or fighting within my head. I thought everyone had that. I thought everyone had the same life I did but it was later revealed that I was very wrong. I'm trying to refigure, rethink, and change that way of thinking.

I've been in therapy for twenty years. I've always thought it was just me being miserable because that's what my mother told me. My whole family system was broken, values and self-esteem were nonexistent. I wanted to die. It was much too painful to deal with the anger, the voices, the fears and dysfunction. I decided to seek therapy for my depression at least for the sake of my girls. I went in and, of course, she did all the background questions about my family and me. She uncovered a world of repressed memories and seventeen different personalities. Dissociative identity disorder involves sections of your mind that have split off, created to hold memories that you can't bear at the time that they happened. That's where it began.

I started developing alternate personalities at a very young age. I had symptoms of eating disorders, relationship problems, flashbacks, nightmares, phobias, and loss of time. This spiraled me into complete submissiveness when it came to the world outside of my mind.

The posttraumatic stress was also caused by being married to someone who hit and degraded me. He was in law enforcement and because of that, nobody would help. This reinforced that the world wasn't a very nice place. He tormented me with mind games and physical abuse. I have scars to remember those times. My neck now has bone spurs that are so bad they narrow my spine. The doctor thought that I had been in a bad accident, and I was too ashamed and embarrassed to tell him that it was from a bad marriage.

I've since had three operations on my back, but the scars on the inside will never heal. They serve as constant reminders that break me down, and I question everything I said, did, and thought, and I wondered why I even existed. One answer for me, was my girls.

The rest of my life is a melting pot of bad choices because I didn't know better. I was taken at gunpoint to another state and narrowly escaped becoming a prostitute. Thank god that guy was caught, but the damage was done, and it added to the list of what-not's and should-not's and what was and what would have been. If I received attention of any kind, no matter what kind, it was better than no attention. I just didn't know any better. I was easily manipulated into being anything and anyone that someone wanted me to be. That led to being raped, and then one of my daughters died.

While I have mental illnesses, I won't give up. I'm a survivor. I broke the cycle for my girls. I raised strong, independent women who are journeying through life.

For me, it's not about finding a cure; there is none. Medications don't work. I will never give up on my dreams, and my spirit will never be broken, although it does have quite a few cracks embedded into it.

*

ERICKA REEVE
Ericka was diagnosed with dissociative identity disorder, posttraumatic stress disorder, obsessive-compulsive disorder, depression, anxiety and an eating disorder in 2013 at age 26

I've struggled for as long as I can recall. I've always had what I once referred to as blackouts. I wouldn't be myself some days. At times, a select few people found this odd and mentioned it to me, but nobody ever really said or did much about it.

I often wondered if I was crazy or going insane. I'm grateful that I eventually found out I am indeed not insane, nor am I a sociopath, sinner, animal or monster; something I was repeatedly told. It was a relief to have an answer to what was occurring throughout my life.

I have always struggled with emotions. They're messy from what I've seen, and despite being able to comprehend the appropriate emotional responses that people have, they still make very little sense to me. I'm currently working on this and trying to understand if it is trauma based or if I may have Asperger's. Either way, I want to know.

Through therapy I, myself, can now tell you more about the early part of my journey. Only a short year ago, this would not have been possible in the way that it is now. I had attempted to find a doctor who could tell me why I was losing such massive amounts of time. I called these instances "blackouts," but came to learn they were so, so much more than that. I wanted to know what was happening to me off and on. Where was I going? What was I doing and how in the world could this continue to occur without anyone being able to answer these questions?

At the age of twenty, one of my parts was raped. My life had so many ups and downs, traumas and inconsistencies already, but they (my parts) thought we were okay, for the most part. Given that my life is a series of unfortunate events, we were again proven wrong. One of my parts was raped by a friend and in our home. This caused a massive uproar within my system. Things were unbelievably chaotic and what had been bad before, became much worse.

We ended up temporarily back with relatives, which only seemed to exacerbate things. Off and on, my parts began moving around quite a bit, but while this was occurring one of them (she's a teenager) began fighting to find us help in a very real way. She could see things were getting even worse, that this other part of me was going to end up killing us or worse. Yes, worse, there are far more sinister things than death.

As this part seemed to push some of her pain aside, she began drinking more and loved to dance. While at a bar in Indiana, she met the man that is now my husband. He is a wonderful, stubborn pain of a man. Loyal and kind, yet rough and gruff. He soothed her. Somehow, some way, he was able to help stabilize her despite having no knowledge of my DID. He was not speaking to me, Erika, but to this fiercely protective part of me, Jynx. He helped. She was at ease and pleased with the distraction.

Only a year or so after they met, I ended up in yet another hospital. I still cannot recall everything that occurred. I was what one would call "switchy", meaning my parts were again thrown into chaos and rapidly switching, coming in and out in attempts to gain control of my body, and over each other in attempts to help the collective group. I know I was at work. I know someone called my husband (then boyfriend) and his mother had dropped me off at the studio that morning.

From there, my next memory is over a month later, and I was living with him. Sure, I knew who he was at that point in the relationship, but I had not known him long enough (in my mind) to move in together. But it was never brought up because I didn't want him to think I was insane like so many others had before him.

When they had taken me to the hospital that day, one of my parts who deals with severe anxiety had been thrust forward and was attempting to deal with things. She was stuck with others who were right there at the surface, and things got tricky and messy. My closest friend came to the hospital to make sure I was okay and upon finding my parents there and my giving them a major tongue lashing—which is completely out of character for me—she said, "You need to leave. She's clearly not herself!" What she was unaware of at the time was just how right she was. The part who was there at that point was Anger, a fierce and aggressive protector. While not at all violent, because she doesn't need to be, Anger is a powerful presence. My future father-in-law had witnessed some of this exchange, or was told of it later, and while I was still switchy (again meaning several were flipping through for control) he said, "Well, you're not going home. You'll live with us." This seemingly small thing to him and his wife had a greater impact than they could ever know. I remember seeing him standing by the window to the left of my hospital bed. My future mother-in-law was sitting beside him on the couch with concern and a touch of fear on her lovely full face. This marked the moment when I wanted to know what was wrong with me.

Fast forward a few years filled with numerous blackouts and several failed doctor visits. My mother had my younger sister beg me to try one more time to see another doctor. I do not remember going or what all occurred during this trip, but my mother and I rented a car and road-tripped down to Florida. I had appointments set up with numerous specialists, one of whom changed my life. He was the head of the neurology department and saw what was happening! He put his theory to the test, and upon being proven right, he found me a referral for a doctor back home. We still see this psychologist today.

I spent over two weeks at the Mayo Clinic and had an extension put on my stay there, not inpatient. I went to a neurologist, remember? A medical doctor. I waited for him to tell me I had an inoperable brain tumor with only months left to live, something I now admit I wanted to hear. While there, I saw countless specialists. I still do not remember my time there, but I have pictures and my mother has talked minimally about it. If my parts weren't as persistent as they were, and this doctor was not who he was, who knows how much longer I would've wandered through life in clouded chaos.

In the years since, we've married and have continued rescuing ferrets. I've been told I can no longer work, but I've been speaking on what it's like living with DID.

*

LORRAINE SCOTT
Lorraine was diagnosed with non-epilepsy attack disorder
and dissociative identity disorder in 2016 at age 48

Life has been good for me, putting to one side traumatic events that I had encountered, illnesses and a couple of failed marriages. I didn't understand and couldn't figure out at times why some things were happening to me. I saw and went through things that no child should ever see or experience, and these traumas from the age of five were what took my childhood. Also, being made to feel like an outcast, an unwanted mistake did not help me either; this pushed all the good away. Sometimes, I had flashbacks of something good or funny, but I couldn't really remember it happening.

I remember having aggressive seizures, but only remember coming out of one. I was constantly having blackouts and spent my life growing up not really understanding what was going on with me.

This was difficult, so I blagged my way through teenage years. As a teenager, I never really knew Lorraine the child. All I can remember are the very bad things she encountered that were no fault of her own. It was, and still is, very frustrating that I can't remember or can't access the good memories. The bad memories have forced the good ones to lock themselves away for safety, so they never get destroyed by the bad ones. One day, I hope that the good will come to the forefront and the bad will be locked away for good.

I managed to get through my teenage years and grew to be a good person, even though I had encountered child abuse, racial abuse, bullying, name-calling and rape. These are just a few examples of what was behind this young girl by the age of fifteen. I attempted suicide twice, something I vowed never to do again as I wanted to value my life. I carried on in life helping others, being a good daughter and friend, and I stood up to bullies. This Lorraine was a very strong one, ready to face whatever was thrown at her; she developed after her second suicide attempt. I wanted to be strong, successful and eventually marry and have children. I continued on this good path. If anything bad knocked me down, I would get up and dust myself off, hold my head high, and carry on. Nothing was going to stop me, and my hopes became my determination.

I completed my schooling and achieved good exam results, although I could have done better if my first couple of years in secondary school were better. I didn't really settle down at school until around age fourteen, but that was a bit too late, as I had missed so much schooling. I couldn't concentrate and would have blackout or absent seizures which made me look incapable of completing tasks. I had to continuously ask the teachers to repeat instructions. Nobody knew that I had been having blackouts and absence seizures, even I didn't know what was going on. My school reports consisted of "Lorraine is easily distracted but can and does produce some good work." I found that I couldn't focus on written tasks except for math, I was brilliant with numbers and brilliant with any practical work.

I went through many different jobs, even ones I never thought I'd have the ability to do, such as teaching. I was successful in all my jobs, even working with and teaching teenage children both in mainstream and in special needs schools. I loved doing this and I was at my happiest, too. Unfortunately, one day while working at a special needs school, I was injured by one of the kids. A month later, I ended up having surgery on my shoulder. This is when other signs of damage to my body started to appear, such as spinal damage along with severe pain. After the operation, I was never to return to that job, as I was told they couldn't keep me safe. I was given another job working as a receptionist and administrator. As time went on, I excelled and was taking on a larger workload. This job was the most relaxed, and so I felt I could enjoy this even more.

The first year flew by, I had gotten to know the characters of the staff, too. At all times, I stayed professional as always and helped where I could to enable a smooth-running day but some people started to make me feel like I wasn't welcome there. Although this was only when they were on duty, it took a toll on me. I was suffering from pain in my spine, neck, and chest and was rushed to the hospital. From this, I was put off work for six months and was barely able to walk. I was finding that I was constantly having blackouts, not knowing what I had done from one day to the next was getting worse. I decided to go and speak to my doctor and explained to him what had been going on. I was now no longer allowed to drive, go swimming or in any pools, ride bikes and was not allowed to be left alone, use any large implements or even cook. I had gone from being very independent to dependent— the biggest flip in my life ever.

I was referred to a neurologist, orthopedist, and spinal surgeon, and then the tests began. From 2010 to 2015, I had an angiogram, full body scan, heart scan, MRI scans of the body and brain, EEGs, ECGs, and video EEG. These led to the diagnoses of three damaged discs in my spine, spinal degeneration, non-epilepsy attack disorder and dissociative identity disorder, known as DID, in 2016.

I didn't realize how much my life was about to change from having the security of a husband, home, job, and my independence to losing all but my kids and home. On top of all that, I married in 2015, and two months later we had to move out of my home of twenty-seven years because of a leak. Me and the kids returned after six months, and the house had been totally renovated.

But I returned as single woman, and my life spiraled downwards to the point of me giving up. I didn't want to get up, go out, or see anyone, I just locked myself away in my room and cried almost all day every day. I never thought that I would come out of the other end, but I did. I was never really going to give up, especially on my children and grandchildren, I was just mourning the abandonment and the feeling of not being wanted anymore by my husband. After divulging my recent diagnosis of DID, it was very hard to take, to understand why someone could be so cruel at a time like this. I thought I would never get over that and his behavior, but I did and I've come out the other side. I've used that major bad experience to inspire me to write and face all my traumas that I have experienced in life. My goal is to have one book with all my stories in to inspire others.

*

CARRIE WORTHINGTON
Carrie was diagnosed with depression,
anxiety, and trichotillomania in 2000 at age 41

Mental illness has been a part of my life since 1991, when my husband was first diagnosed with bipolar. I learned that there wasn't a lot of resources for people and a lot of stigma, so I became his biggest advocate.

Living with mental illness every day is the unknown. I would wake up not knowing what the day would bring, if the meds would have my husband Robin stable or if he would be manic. With his illness, it was best that he become a stay-at-home dad. He took his role seriously and it was a very amicable life for us.

Soon after moving into our home, our son was diagnosed with bipolar and ADHD. Even with his illness, Robin and I worked together to try to deal with this new twist. Soon after this, the pressure of being the stable one started to affect me. Soon I was not as organized as I had been or I would ignore mail because it seemed too much to handle. I started pulling out my hair, which relieved the anxiety. I didn't face the fact that I, too, was mentally ill. I couldn't be, I was the strong one. For years, I had been advocating for better coverage, continued to learn and read everything I could on care, meds, support, doctors, etc. I was diagnosed with depression and trichotillomania, and put on antidepressants and anxiety medication.

Years later, I became the go-to person when someone was facing a sudden mental health crisis. I assisted many families and helped them get through by answering questions, providing information, and just helping them to deal with it. I was happy to do this, as I did not have this support ten years earlier.

I became involved with NAMI Will-Grundy. Within six months, I was president and set out to help re-vamp the business process and improve the programs. I kept very busy and distracted, but it was fulfilling to me. One day in 2010, I decided to do something drastic to change my life. I weighed over three hundred pounds, so I started the process of getting a full gastric bypass. At the time I made this decision, my depression was the worst it ever was. I did not handle decisions well. I did not deal with the fact that my son and husband were both off their meds and very ill, and I did not realize my husband and I were drifting apart. I decided to do this surgery to help my life.

The surgery went well and my husband took very good care of me. A few months later, after the pounds were falling off, I was feeling so good and wanted to go off all medication. I stopped the anti-depressants and gradually stopped the Paxil. Four days after taking the final Paxil tablet I passed out at work. The emergency room staff didn't care that I told them five times that I had taken my last Paxil four days before. I had every physical test and was then released as "being dizzy." Over the weekend, I grew worse. I looked up Paxil withdrawal and I had twenty of the twenty-five possible side effects. I immediately called the psychiatric ward at the local hospital and was told that unless I was suicidal, there was nothing I could do.

My head was literally buzzing with what felt like zapping electrical waves. I was dizzy, my equilibrium was absent, and I knew there was something seriously wrong. I called my general practitioner and the doctor on staff prescribed a high blood pressure medicine and valium. The high blood pressure medication eventually stopped the zapping. Two days later, I wasn't doing that well. I laid in bed and felt like there were ants crawling in my brain. I picked up the clock-radio and started to try to kill them. My husband came in, grabbed it out of my hands, and called the ambulance. I spent four days in the hospital, and was off work for six weeks. I was going through severe Paxil withdrawal. I had psychosis, and had no idea what I was doing. In my mind, I was really okay. The only thing I was very aware of was that I couldn't read. I saw the letters, I knew what they were, but could not put them together to form a word. I couldn't read. I knew this was bad.

Eventually I started to come back. I did not know what I was doing, but I knew I wasn't right. Later I was told I was mean, slurred my words, and sometimes did not make sense. Four weeks after I returned to work, my husband passed away. It was five days before Christmas.

I went through the next six weeks like it was a dream. I functioned, but was supported by good friends, and my daughter moved back in with me. For the next year, my daughter lived with me, taking care of most things around the house until I slowly adjusted to doing it myself.

I had five major changes in my life in a twelve-month period, including losing my job of sixteen years, after which I started having panic attacks. My therapist tried to convince me to go back on medication. I fought it for two years but then decided to take my antidepressants and Xanax.

Three years later, I received news about a decision involving my granddaughter. My mind broke; it felt like it had cracked. I called my friend. My friend sat with me until I could see my therapist. I knew I had to be there to talk to him, as I knew I just didn't want to go on. Thirty minutes into the session, I mentioned that I was afraid because I had to face the weekend alone. He asked me "Can you promise me you will be safe?" The most honest thing I have ever done was say "No." I knew at that point he couldn't let me leave. It took him awhile to coax me into being evaluated, and I was admitted to the psych unit. The experience was scary at first but it was what I needed; it was a time out. I could step back and really examine where I had come from, and where I was now. In addition to learning what was important for me, it again turned out to be an experience I could use in my advocacy for mental illness.

For the last two years, I have not had one thought or ideation of suicide. I know in my heart that it will never be the answer. Adjusting to being alone (my daughter moved out) is so foreign, as I have never lived alone.

About three years after my husband's death, I started to feel like moving forward. I found another job that was better suited for me and I have started the slow process of learning a new life. The depression sets me back sometimes, but I continue to work at it. I'm still in therapy and continue to learn that I am not the bad thoughts or the sad feelings, but rather a strong woman who has survived and will continue to survive. The depression is always there, but lately I feel like I have been coming out on top. I am now able to cope and handle changes that come up in a very healthy and positive way. I recognize thoughts and feelings, but they do not take control of me. I am now taking control of them. For a long time I had no idea of how to care for myself. I'm now, almost good at it.

*

# CHAPTER TWO

# Suspecting the Truth

After all these years, I am still involved in the process of self-discovery. It's better to explore life and make mistakes than to play it safe. -SOPHIA LOREN

Long before the diagnosis, we have an inkling that something is different and inherently search for answers as to why we act, feel, or react in the ways we do. Instinctively, we turn inward and explore our inner psyche on our path to self-discovery. When did you first suspect you had a mental illness?

*

ADRIANNE ALLEN-LANG
Adrianne was diagnosed with dissociative identity disorder in 2015 at age 18

It's hard to explain here, because I never really knew I had an illness or that something was wrong with me until I was a young teenager. But as a child, in looking back now, I always had signs of mental illness.

I can't say when I first noticed exactly, but the earliest I remember is being about five or six years old and sitting in the game room at my father's house. He had bought my brother and I a remote control light-up UFO that we could fly around. I couldn't sleep and had gotten up at some early hour and was playing with it in the game room. I remember hearing voices saying how fun the UFO was, and to make it go higher and if we made it hit the light, it would make fireworks. I never did fly the UFO into the light, but from then on I have memories of my voices helping me through school and playing with me, but also putting me down. They started encouraging suicide when I was eleven, after my father had missed my birthday.

Finally getting my diagnosis was a relief. I had done a lot of personal research and soul-searching to find answers for what was happening inside my mind. A diagnosis didn't help in any way, besides enabling me to access correct treatment options, but for me it was like a weight had been lifted off my shoulders. It meant that what I was experiencing was real and valid, and that I wasn't alone.

*

MORGAN BUTLER
Morgan was diagnosed with depression
and anxiety in 2009 at age 15

I'm not sure if there was a specific moment when I realized that I probably had depression. My entire childhood was a roller coaster, with my mother tugging at my heartstrings and the disappointment that came along with unfulfilled promises. I had emotional outbursts when I finally moved in with my father and stepmom permanently. I was usually sweet and shy in class, but I would have moments of high anxiety where I'd just hide under my desk, this was in second and third grade. I'd get angry for no reason, and be rude, even to my friends. However, this could have been the transition causing my uncharacteristic moodiness.

Around middle school, in 2005 and 2006, there was a big musical movement of the "emo" genre, where they talked about cutting and otherwise, and suddenly I connected with it all. Not just as a movement, but on a personal level. All those years of having to be strong and bottle up my emotions to be the happy, sweet girl who my family prided me as, were finally taking their toll. I began to self-harm, and become more reserved, at home especially.

In 2009, one of my parents found my journal. I won't be too explicit about my thoughts, but they found out about my cutting, and immediately they were overwhelmed and forced me to the doctor to refer us to a counselor.

At this point in time, I was numb, and I didn't want much to do with someone who didn't know me. However, I knew that I needed to do this to make my stepmom feel better. I wasn't surprised at the diagnosis, considering I'd been like that for years; I knew what was going on but I didn't want the help, and kept it hidden.

\*

LYNDA CHELDELIN FELL
Lynda was diagnosed with depression in 2000 at age 35
and posttraumatic stress disorder in 2012 at age 47

For years, I never thought of depression as a mental illness. To my mind, mental illness was something entirely different, something I didn't have. Maybe I didn't consider my depression as a mental illness because I wasn't bedridden with it like my great-grandmother was. Of course I wasn't; I am one of thousands who benefit from medication that wasn't around in her time. But had it not been for medication, without a shadow of a doubt the illness would have crippled me.

Perhaps I was too proud to accept the diagnosis of mental illness. After all, mental illness was something that happened to other people, like the homeless, not highly functioning people like me. I now know that mental illness isn't discriminatory, and can happen to anyone.

To answer the question of when I first realized I had depression, it came on the heels of the collapse of my first marriage. With two young children and the discovery that my husband was leading two lives, I felt trapped. I was a good girl who hadn't nary a blemish to my name. Raised in a family where name was everything, I felt caught between a dead-end marriage and feeling like I had made my bed with this man, and I had better lie in it. I sunk into a terrible depression, and felt hopeless in life. Because I thought it was the right thing to do, after all we had two children, I convinced my husband to attend marriage counseling with me. It was a fiasco because the therapist was another female which he could bed. And he did. And she did. I left.

I knew I was severely depressed but never sought medical treatment at the time because Prozac had just come on the market and was highly stigmatized. Also, in my world, good girls didn't take Prozac. Divorce too was stigmatized, but my husband left me with no option. I wasn't willing to continue to live a lie. And so I bore the scarlet D in a world and family where divorce was considered scandalous. At least my children would be safe.

Thankfully, the depression lifted as the marriage dissolved. I then went on to meet Mr. Right and the love of my life. Beauty returned to my world as he fell in love with me and my two small children, and we with him. It would be nearly ten years before I suffered my next bout, which was the first one actually diagnosed. By that time, I knew what I had and was more receptive to getting proper treatment. My life depended upon it.

*

SHAUNA COX
Shauna was diagnosed with an
anxiety disorder in 2009 at age 26

Ever since I was a kid, I have been considered a "worrier." I would worry about small things like an essay I had to write for school, and I would worry about big things like my parents dying. Sometimes, I would worry so intensely that I would start to cry, or I would feel nauseous or have diarrhea. I often avoided such things as parties or giving speeches in class, and my parents just figured I was really shy. Well, I am shy, but it turned out to be more than just that.

From my psychology background in university, I knew that I had some of the symptoms of an anxiety disorder, but I never let myself believe that I truly fit the criteria. Up until my diagnosis at the age of twenty-six, I just thought that I was on the far edge of normal when it came to feeling anxious. I knew that I tended to worry more than other people, and I was always overthinking and overanalyzing everything, but surely that wasn't a result of a mental illness, was it?

When I was twenty-five, my husband, Roger, and I moved to St. Paul, Alberta from Brampton, Ontario in 2008, so I could start a new career working with individuals with disabilities. The job itself wasn't what I had anticipated, and I came home crying almost every day thinking that we had made a horrible decision moving across the country. I quit and took a job at a funeral home as an administrative assistant. I was much happier there, but my anxiety started to go through the roof. I was on edge every day, worrying about everything.

If Roger went out and was later than anticipated coming home, I would immediately jump to thinking that he had been in a car accident. If I called him and he didn't answer, my fears would be confirmed in my head and I would think the worst. He would inevitably show up five minutes later to find me hysterically crying.

I also started to experience anxiety whenever I was left alone at work, and not because of the ghosts! I started to fear being put in a position where I was the only one in the building to answer phones or greet clients. What if I had to run to the bathroom? What if I waited because I couldn't leave to go to the bathroom and had an accident?

Around this time, I started to become fearful of going shopping and being in line by myself for the same reason, and made Roger come with me wherever I went. I was also now experiencing diarrhea and nausea on more days than not because of the anxiety. The fight or flight instinct was kicking in, and my body was deciding on flight. When I called in sick for work because of this, I knew I had to seek help. Enough was enough. I called a psychologist and made an appointment for the following day.

Going to see a psychologist was the best thing I could have done! While my suspicion that I had an anxiety disorder was confirmed, my psychologist also helped me work through different fears, and helped me develop strategies to overcome them. I was able to see how some of my concerns were irrational, and I learned how to let go of the worries about situations that I can't control. Recognizing that I had a mental illness was the first real step in dealing with the problem and in finding ways to get better.

\*

JANE MCDONALD
Jane was diagnosed with major depressive disorder in 1989,
multiple anxiety disorders in 2001, multiple personality
disorders in 2007, and dissociative identity disorder in 2014

Long before I was diagnosed, I felt that I was different from other kids my age. They seemed to always (or most of the time) be happy and carefree, whereas I was profoundly sad and anxious. I knew that a large part of this was a result of the bullying that I endured but I also just figured I was just overly sensitive. I could be upset by the smallest things. Honestly, I just put it down to having a disposition more like my father, who suffered from depression (unbeknownst to me until a later age). I was always serious, always worrying about something or another, always despairing of my life. Honestly, I figured it was a normal reaction to what I was going through: bullying, verbal and sexual abuse, parental neglect. I didn't know what I was going through had a label, that it was an actual diagnosis and that there was treatment for it. I figured it was the way my life was meant to be, and I resigned myself to feelings of profound sadness and heightened anxiety.

At the time of my first diagnosis, I remember my doctor going through the signs and symptoms of clinical depression and thinking "Yep, that's me." I wasn't really surprised by it because it was how I had been feeling for most of my life. The idea that it was something that could be treated was somewhat of a relief. I was too cautious to hold out much hope though. I had felt like this all my life and didn't really believe I could ever feel anything different.

Once I reached high school and had a better grasp of what it truly meant to have depression, I started to experience a number of different emotions. By this time, I found out that my father and grandmother both had the same diagnosis. I found it to be a relief that it wasn't just me who had went through this. It also felt like maybe there was a valid reason that I had it, namely that I had inherited it from my father's side of the family. This made me feel like my depression was legitimate and not just a result of personal weaknesses and failures, as my mother made me feel it was. If anything, I felt closer to my father and grandmother knowing that they, too, were going through similar things to what I was going through.

When I received the further diagnoses of my anxiety disorders in university, I remember feeling relieved but also confused. The social anxiety disorder and general anxiety disorder were understandable. I was easily able to trace it back to the bullying I had received as a child, both at the hands of classmates as well as family members and so-called family "friends." The general anxiety disorder just meant that I had a propensity toward anxiety which, honestly, made sense. It actually surprised me that it had taken as long as it had to receive these diagnoses. PTSD was a bit more difficult to accept. I always associated PTSD with war veterans who had fought in the trenches and suffered a nervous breakdown of sorts. I was no such person. What trauma had I experienced that was so severe as to cause PTSD? With time, I have gradually come to accept this diagnosis along with the others.

The next diagnosis that confused me and caught me off-guard was that of borderline personality disorder. Before my actual diagnosis in 2007, it had been suggested to me by one of my psychology professors. Although it was not officially diagnosed until many years later, after I left university, it was something which, as I did more and more research on it, seemed to explain a lot of what I was feeling and experiencing. This new label was more difficult to accept. Part of this was because I knew so little about it. There was also confusion about why, if this was the case (which it certainly seemed to be the more I learned about it), why had no one mentioned or even suggested it to me? Why had none of my therapists ever suggested this, while a psychology professor who didn't know me half as well was able to pick up on it? This was more than a little disappointing and frustrating. At this point in my life, I wasn't looking for any more diagnoses, any more labels. But there it was. It was hard to deny that it could be true. The intensity of emotions, the difficulties with sense of identity, the shifting values, the dissociation. But again, nothing was made official until many years later when I was diagnosed with not just borderline personality disorder but also avoidant personality disorder and dependent personality disorder.

As I said, these labels were a bit harder to accept. Stigma was a real thing for me now. While depression and anxiety were far more well-known and common place, a personality disorder, let alone three, were not as common or as well understood. To my mind, it meant that something was seriously wrong with me, with who I was at the core of my being. Something was intrinsically wrong with the very fundamental aspects of who I was, with my personality. This wasn't something a pill could fix. And that scared me. I could take antianxiety and depression meds and get a bit better. There was no pill to fix a dysfunctional personality.

To have not just one, but three personality disorders was even more difficult to swallow. As I did more research and came to realize that these were accurate diagnoses, it became more and more terrifying. How did this go unnoticed for so long? Were my depression and anxiety real or were they just a symptom of these personality disorders?

My most recent diagnosis was the most difficult to accept of all: dissociative identity disorder. It had never occurred to me despite all of my years of studying psychology and mental illness. I knew I had certain symptoms, I knew I felt like I had "others" inside of my head, but I had never put two and two together that this might be what that all meant. This was, to me, perhaps one of the least understood, much misaligned diagnoses in the DSM. The portrayals of those with DID in the media didn't help matters. People with DID were seen as crazy and needed to be locked up in mental institutions. Again, much like personality disorders, there was something fundamentally wrong with me which no amount of mediation could cure. Even with therapy, the chances of recovery are not great. With intense treatment over the course of several years, some patients can integrate their personalities and learn to live as one person, but in essence you are always someone with DID. It doesn't go away. That is a terrifying prospect for someone like me who, at this point in my life and with so many mental health diagnoses, would do anything to just be normal.

I was diagnosed with DID two years ago, but although it was hinted at by a previous psychiatrist, I was never told about this. That in itself led to a lot of outrage and frustration. Regardless, I am two years into this diagnosis and although there is still a lot of denial, I am learning to live with it along with my other mental health diagnoses.

Having a health problem of any sort is difficult, but we all have to find a way to live with these diagnoses and do the best we can. That is really all anyone can ask of us.

\*

AMY OWEN
Amy was diagnosed with ADD and
bipolar disorder in 2014 at age 42

I was in my early thirties. I felt angry, alone, confused, but mostly disappointed. I couldn't talk to anyone because no one in my family believed in any mental illness. They just thought it was me being difficult. They still think it isn't real and that I can just change. I was so ashamed of myself. I felt broken and like an outcast. I didn't want to be different. I didn't want to worry the rest of my life about being mentally ill. But mostly, I worried about my kids having this and what they would go through. It makes me sad to think that they could have this too.

\*

AMBER PILLARS
Amber was diagnosed with
schizophrenia in 2004 at age 24

It took me years and years to accept help for my undiagnosed depression. I had begun taking antidepressants in December 2004, but I was convinced that I was only depressed. The doctors, my coworkers, my family, and my friends all knew my condition was more than depression. I refused any medicine but antidepressants because the first family medicine doctor I went to told me the diagnosis. That diagnosis was depression. I was also the kind of person who took ibuprofen only when absolutely necessary. I didn't put any medicine in my body unless it was necessary. So, it was very hard for me to take antidepressants.

It wasn't until February 2005, at age twenty-four, when I realized it was more than depression. I had been transferred to my third hospital within two months. At that time, I was committed to the mental health unit in the hospital and was forced to take antipsychotic medicine by injections. I am not even sure what medicines they gave me, I know they tried quite a few. Everyone around me knew I needed it, but my mind was too far gone to realize it.

The moment I realized I needed the antipsychotic medicine was the day I called my parents to come visit right away. They came quickly. I was scared and knew something was wrong with me. I tried walking up and down the hall, but my muscles cramped up in unnatural ways and I couldn't move. I remember Pope John Paul II was on the news, as he was failing and about ready to die. I was scared I was dying, too. I remember my parents were in the hallway when my whole body cramped and twisted in unnatural ways. I was not able to move. My parents yelled for the nurse and I told the nurse I would take whatever I needed to now, without refusing. I was so frightened because it felt like I was failing and going to die.

I found out later that the muscles cramping up was called a dystonic reaction from the antipsychotic medicines. They had given me too much for my body weight, as I was a really tiny young lady. I remember telling a doctor at a different hospital that even non-drowsy cold medicine knocked me out. I was trying to tell him my body is affected easily by medicines.

In looking back, the fact that doctors gave me too much actually saved my life, because that's the reason why I had a dystonic reaction. And because of that dystonic reaction, I realized I needed to take my antipsychotic medicines as well as my antidepressant medicines.

\*

DENISE PURCELL
Denise was diagnosed with depression, posttraumatic stress
disorder, and dissociative identity disorder in 1995 at age 30

When I felt helpless and alone and my life was falling apart, I had nightmares and flashbacks and couldn't focus. I went to a therapist, my first one, because of a failed marriage. The second was for an eating disorder, the third was for dissociative identity disorder, PTSD, and complex depression. I was relieved to find out, because I knew something wasn't right with me. I sought help but was overwhelmed with the diagnoses, especially with the last bunch. I didn't understand them, and thought it would be a quick fix.

\*

ERICKA REEVE
Ericka was diagnosed with dissociative identity disorder,
posttraumatic stress disorder, obsessive-compulsive disorder,
depression, anxiety and an eating disorder in 2013 at age 26

I'm uncertain of the exact day or time, but I know when I was young I always felt something wasn't quite right. My parts had met our therapist long before I ever did. My initial reaction was likely uncertainty, confusion, a touch of realization and understanding, coupled with relief. I think the relief and a few other emotions were more so, me feeling my parts, but I know relief was a big one across the board for us. Finally, there was an answer.

Now through years of therapy, I do have additional diagnoses, but that is common when dealing with dissociative identity disorder. PTSD and OCD were two of the earlier added diagnoses, along with depression and anxiety.

*

LORRAINE SCOTT
Lorraine was diagnosed with non-epilepsy attack disorder
and dissociative identity disorder in 2016 at age 48

I was officially diagnosed in 2016 with non-epilepsy attack disorder (NEAD) and dissociative identity disorder (DID) at age forty-eight. After the previous six years, I was finally diagnosed and happy to know what had been wrong with me all my life. I was so relieved and I now I understood myself, and why I have lost some of my memories of my childhood.

When I first learned that I was and had been living with DID, I left the hospital with a big fat question mark over my head. I was told to go home and research it, and on my next visit I could tell them what I thought and we could discuss any issue or concerns that I had. So, once I got in the taxi for a twenty-minute drive home, I was straight on the phone googling DID. I spent the next couple of days researching and completing online tests. I was astonished with the results of the tests, stating that there was a great possibility that I had DID. These tests are/were just for informational purposes and not a real diagnosis. Although I had already been diagnosed, they helped with pointing out signs and would refer me to go see my general practitioner.

When I was reading about this, it was like "OMG, this is me down to a tee." I could honestly say I ticked eighty-five to ninety out of a hundred questions. It was shocking that I could relate to so much of what I was reading. I was like "Yep, this is me," or "OMG, I thought I was going crazy," or "Wow, I can't believe what I'm reading." This all gave me a sense of relief and wholesomeness, for once I finally understood myself and the things others said that I had done or said that I don't have any memory of. For once in my life, I felt complete; it was like someone opened the dark door that was blocking the light.

I had also been waiting for five years for a diagnosis as to why I was having seizures, "conking" out, having blackouts, memory loss, and more. After going through all the tests, in January 2016, I was diagnosed with nonepileptic attack disorder. In April 2016, I was diagnosed with dissociative identity disorder.

When I was a child, I experienced grand mal seizures, but don't ever remember being diagnosed. I only remember coming out of one. My mother was very upset, as it was Boxing Day. The doctor who tended to me was drunk, and my mom was scared that something bad was going to happen to me. I remember her crying and kicking the doctor out of the house. I could hear everything but also hadn't fully come around before having another seizure. This is the only seizure that I have any memory of coming out of, even though it was just a few seconds before I began to seize again. I have no other memories of that seizure, or of all the others over the years.

Through my teenage and adult years, the seizures continued but in different forms. When I was diagnosed, I hadn't heard of it until the neurologist mentioned that it could be stress-related seizures. I couldn't understand how stress could cause seizures, but it's amazing what I've learned. My seizures were caused by daily mental and physical stressors. My feelings weren't too bad to start off with, but it did take some understanding as to why my body would react like this to different types of stress. After a few days of this sinking in, the tears and other emotions set in.

Once I had been diagnosed with both illnesses, eventually I went numb. I didn't know what to think. I went from being happy to sad;

relief turned into tears of fear, sadness, and shame. But overall it was a relief to be diagnosed because it had been going on for so many years, and not knowing what is wrong with you is one of the most awful experiences ever. I went through so many different emotions. I worried I was going crazy; others around me worried the same.

A friend of mine, I'll call him Sam, gave me permission to add his thoughts throughout this book, as he has mental illnesses and we discuss and support each other as needed. He had three missed diagnoses of bipolar, schizophrenia and psychosis at age sixteen. He acted out aggressively and had difficulties with family life, too. He reached out to his general practitioner for help, which later led to his diagnoses. When I asked him how it made him feel and what emotions he went through, he said that due to the lack of knowledge on these illnesses and fear brought upon him by others in the family who also had mental illness, his relationship with his father became extremely difficult, fragile, and violent. He didn't feel relieved knowing that there was a reason behind his actions/behavior, but he feared what the future held. As time passed, he felt that he wasn't going to let that break him down and found ways to channel his emotions and decisions into constructive activities that were beneficial to him. This allowed him to take control of his life and not allow labels of illnesses and the negativity that they can bring destroy him.

This shows how we all take and see things differently, although some of our emotions can still be linked.

\*

CARRIE WORTHINGTON
Carrie was diagnosed with depression,
anxiety, and trichotillomania in 2000 at age 41

When I first started to be the breadwinner after my husband's breakdown, I started pulling out my hair. I was anxious and worried about being able to be the one who could support my family; I felt a huge amount of pressure. Pulling my hair, and the physical pain for every hair that was pulled, helped deal with this feeling. When I realized I had bald patches and it was now a habit, I became extremely embarrassed. I didn't deal with my trichotillomania until I spoke with my general practitioner. It took two or three years for me to even look it up, to see what was going on and put a name to it. In a way, I was relieved to know there was a name, and that I wasn't alone.

I once mentioned it to a doctor who looked at me and said, "No, you don't." Just like that, it was dismissed even though at that time it was one of the hardest things I had ever had to admit. It took me a few years of changing doctors and speaking to a new, trusted doctor. I told him, "I pull my hair out."

He looked at me and said "Oh, trichotillomania."

No judgment, just trust that I knew what I was talking about. We discussed several medications and he started me on Paxil.

The difference between the two doctors and their reactions was, at that point, the exact culture of denying mental illness. Even though I had a name, a doctor I could talk to, and medication to help, to this day I have still never spoken to anyone except immediate family about this part of my mental illness. I still feel shame, and I'm sure they wonder why half of my head has less hair than the other side.

Thankfully, after many years of therapy, this is now a very rare occurrence. I use tools to help and have learned not to sit and obsess, worry, and be anxious about things that are going on. As for my depression, I remember a time when, unlike my previous abilities, I started to become unorganized, and ill-prepared. I just felt like things were starting to become overwhelming. Soon, I saw other things that I hadn't been dealing with such as paying bills and opening mail, because it just seemed too much. When I felt like something was going on, I went into total denial. Not me—I couldn't be mentally ill. My husband and my son had mental illness, but I couldn't be mentally ill too. I was the caregiver, I kept everything together.

I was in such deep denial that I refused to go to the family psychiatrist. Instead, I went to my trusted general practitioner for treatment. With his assistance, I started to let the reality of my own mental illness sink in.

*

CHAPTER THREE

# The Shadow of Stigma

People say I'm unique, that there aren't others with schizophrenia like me. Well, there are people like me out there, but the stigma is so great that they don't come forward. -ELYN SAKS

Mental illness is a disease in the shadows, and many are reluctant to admit such a thing— even to close family and friends—because of the stigma. It immediately sets us apart from others. Fearing a negative reaction, many of us aren't comfortable openly discussing our illness. Do you tell people about your mental illness?

\*

ADRIANNE ALLEN-LANG
Adrianne was diagnosed with dissociative
identity disorder in 2015 at age 18

I tell people close to me about my mental illness but unless people follow my blogging or those who know me well, they don't usually suspect anything and I often get a surprised reaction of "But you don't look so sick!" For everything except my DID, most people are understanding and respectful. But when it comes to DID, people often assume psychosis and get scared. That's not their fault, that's just ignorance and media washing, so I try to be as open as I can about my experiences to try to break the stigmas surrounding my illnesses.

For a long time, I was really ashamed of what I was experiencing. I could never figure out why people didn't think the way I did, or feel so passionately and strongly about everything like me. Being open and learning to become a therapist has really helped me come to acceptance with my diagnosis.

\*

MORGAN BUTLER
Morgan was diagnosed with depression
and anxiety in 2009 at age 15

Nowadays, I am an open book and huge advocate for stomping out the stigma that revolves around depression, anxiety, and suicide. Most people are respectful about me being borderline-outspoken on the issue, but I have found some people (even some of whom I've dated) that can't understand it because they've never experienced or witnessed anything relative to my mental illness. The biggest thing is understanding that some people just won't get it, and you can't get too mad at them. When you're not having a low, you have to try to tell them how they can support you when you are having a hard time with your illness, you know? Otherwise, they may not have the right tools to support you. Most people I know try and reach out and be supportive. Since I'm in good control of it now, I've tried to be more of an advocate for others.

*

LYNDA CHELDELIN FELL
Lynda was diagnosed with depression in 2000 at age 35
and posttraumatic stress disorder in 2012 at age 47

Once upon a time, I told my mother I had developed a fondness for shopping in secondhand stores. To me it was like a treasure hunt, and I excitedly exclaimed how much fun it was to search through another person's trinkets that might prove to be my treasure. Oh, goodness, what in the world? My mother quickly admonished doing such a thing out of fear someone might see me. Secondhand stores were for poor people. What might our neighbors think?

That was a lesson in just how powerful stigma can be. My mother was raised by my grandmother, a poor but loving widow left alone to fend for her five children. My mother knew all about being poor, and she wasn't having it for her own children. And so I hid my new hobby in the shadows, safe from judgmental eyes and opinions. And I learned to do the same for depression.

Over the past eight years, the heartaches I've faced have corrected my life priorities. I've become much more open about many things, including mental illness. If we don't work together to raise awareness and remove stigmas, future generations will inherit the same shame and fears. I don't want that for my children and grandchildren.

Mental illness isn't something we asked to have. It isn't something we earned as a consequence of our actions. Yet, some still judge me because of it. What does depression mean? Am I stable? Am I a danger to be around? Will I go postal? It will continue to disgrace and discredit us all if we don't take a stand to correct the urban legends surrounding the myths. Somebody has to set the dialogue straight, and it might as well be us.

*

SHAUNA COX
Shauna was diagnosed with an
anxiety disorder in 2009 at age 26

Once I get to know people, I am open about my anxiety disorder. I believe that the stigma surrounding mental illness needs to be wiped away, and the only way this will happen is if people are open about their illnesses and share what they go through on a daily basis. I've found that people tend to be surprised but incredibly understanding when they find out about my disorder. They also seem to be interested in learning more about my diagnosis, what I experience, and what I have done in the way of treatments. Through my openness, I've met people going through some of the same issues or who know others who have the same diagnosis. They're often impressed by my willingness to talk about what I go through, and genuinely curious at the same time.

I've never felt compelled to hide that I have an anxiety disorder, perhaps because when I do share with others, I feel a sense of safety. It helps to know that the people around me know what I'm going through, because I can then ask and gain their support in ways that I might not have otherwise. People constantly amaze me with their understanding and support, and I often feel that I wouldn't have progressed as far as I have without the people in my life helping me.

*

JANE MCDONALD
Jane was diagnosed with major depressive disorder in 1989,
multiple anxiety disorders in 2001, multiple personality
disorders in 2007, and dissociative identity disorder in 2014

Revealing that you have a mental illness is always an intensely personal decision. Despite the recent attention from the Bell Canada "Let's Talk" campaign, which encourages everyone with mental health issues to talk to their friends and family about their diagnoses, many people still legitimately fear the repercussions of doing so.

I remember growing up in a household where the expression of any emotions was severely looked down upon. My mother spoke of my father's depression as if it were the plague, thus highly stigmatizing mental illness in my mind. I grew to learn that mental illness was not something that you spoke about, neither at home nor outside of the home. My mom was always concerned with how the family appeared to those on the outside and prided herself on the appearance of having the perfect family. Thus, I learned from a young age to keep any of my mental illnesses a secret, as if they were signs of weakness. It has taken me many years to fight this stigma and to learn to be more open about all aspects of my personality, including my mental health issues.

However, how much I share often depends on the person and the context of the conversation. Many days I am thankful that mental illness is an invisible disability, and that people can't tell just from looking at me that I am mentally ill.

For me, telling anyone about my mental illness is complicated because of the fact that I have so many diagnoses. While I feel comfortable telling most people that I have some form of mental illness, I often leave out the details as to how many diagnoses I have and even which diagnoses they are. For years, my family has known that I have depression and anxiety, but when I received the diagnoses of having different personality disorders, I felt I had to keep these a secret. One of the factors that led to that decision was the fact that even a cursory knowledge of personality disorders and DID will tell you that they are often caused by childhood trauma. I didn't want to tell my parents that I had these diagnoses as I didn't want them to blame themselves or, more accurately, to think I was blaming them. I even kept it from my sister because I feared that she would think I was "faking it," because there was no severe childhood trauma that either of us can recall (although we both have little recollection of our youngest years, before around the age of five). Unfortunately, when I was in a treatment program for my personality disorders, my family ended up asking a lot of questions about why I wasn't able to visit or spend certain days with them. I tried to explain I was taking some psychology courses to further my education, but they didn't buy that explanation. Eventually, I confessed that I had a personality disorder although I didn't say there were three of them, nor which ones they were. While my mom doesn't talk much about that stuff, whenever I visit my dad and stepmom, they always seem to walk on eggshells around me and are overly concerned with how I am doing. This is exactly the behavior and attitudes I was afraid of. I know they mean well but I wished they realized they didn't have to do that, that I am still the same daughter they've always had. As a result of the negative reaction to my personality disorders, I have kept my DID diagnosis from all of my family.

When it came to telling my friends about my mental illness it was a whole other matter. One main factor in this was that, frankly, I never had many close friends growing up and I still don't. In elementary school and high school, people could tell that I was unhappy and anxious, so it was not something I felt I needed to talk about. In university, I chose to remain isolated and only had a very few close friends. Although one of the reasons for this was that I am naturally very shy and introverted, another reason was that I purposely tried to keep to myself. I was afraid of making friends and having them learn about my mental illness and reject me or judge me for it, as my few friends in elementary school had done. Eventually, I did get close to a few people, and although I tried to keep my illness to myself, I began having depressive episodes and panic attacks while in their company. Some friends did leave me but some also stayed and tried their best to help me and accept me, regardless of my disorders.

As an adult, I again was left with few friends after moving to a new city to escape an abusive relationship. There was a small group of about five people who I did become friends with but we met, of all places, in a treatment program for personality disorders. Therefore, they were well aware that I had a personality disorder but I kept from them the specific ones, as well as the fact that there were multiple diagnoses. I also kept my DID a secret from them for a long time, although recently I've opened up about it to a couple of them. I found them to be very understanding and curious about what it means and how I cope with it.

In terms of work and school, I have had to reveal to my employer and teachers that I had a mental illness as I thought it might affect me in those settings. Both my employer and former teachers were very accepting and accommodating, which was a relief. With my employer I let her know that I had other personalities because I feared that someone else might come out at work and I would be unable to do my job. This has in fact, happened on occasion, and my boss is able to set me aside on my own, give me small tasks to keep me occupied, and wait until I've settled down and am able to function. If the other personality takes over for the entire time I am at work (which fortunately is only a few hours), she knows that I need to be kept busy with puzzles and such. I feel that revealing mental illness to employers, in particular, can be extremely difficult and I am fortunate that my employer is more than willing to work with me and accommodate me rather than immediately dismiss me, as many do these days for people with varying mental illnesses.

*

AMY OWEN
Amy was diagnosed with ADD and
bipolar disorder in 2014 at age 42

I tell very few people. Only friends I know who will not judge me. Only family that I know would not look at me different. I have told a few coworkers I have depression but not bipolar disorder. I am ashamed when I tell others. I feel like I'm being judged and I worry I'll lose my job and people I care about. I have one friend I can talk to that makes me feel safe, and I can tell her anything without shame.

*

AMBER PILLARS
Amber was diagnosed with
schizophrenia in 2004 at age 24

It's a very tricky part of my life to bring up with new friends, dates, coworkers and bosses. Within two to three years of my major episode, I was super willing to share some details with the new people in my life. It could be as simple as sharing that I was doing research studies for mental health locally and nationally. Sometimes, I would share more details like my diagnosis of schizophrenia.

I had a group of young adult friends from church (new friends since the diagnosis) with whom I shared with more details. They were, and still are, a huge blessing in my life. They treated me no different than anyone else. They became my support to still having a social life. I will be forever grateful to them.

At that time, the church made a video spotlighting my story. I talked about my mental illness and recovery. I had started going on a couple of dates with this amazing guy from my sand volleyball team and church. I thought he would probably see the video at church eventually, so I shared with him that I was diagnosed with a mental illness of schizophrenia. Though it was only our second date, I felt he deserved to know before he saw it at church.

I told him during the middle of our date. And by the end of the date, I could tell there was not going to be another date. I feel that part of the reason was because he wasn't ready to handle that kind of information. It's nothing against him, he is still a great guy. It's just a lot for a person to take in if they don't know you very well yet. It made me feel sad and heartbroken. I am definitely more careful now about how and when I tell guys I am dating of my circumstances.

I will sometimes share a small bit with coworkers and bosses. But I also learned the hard way that the boss may hold it against me later on. I am scared to share things at work. Because they may use it against me if I make one mistake. I am now way more careful how I share that I know about mental illness. I don't always tell them it's me that has dealt with it directly.

Sometimes, God has other plans for me. I have become good friends with an old coworker. I shared with him that I was diagnosed with schizophrenia twelve years ago. He has taught me that if someone cares for me enough, he/she will see me for me and not for my mental illness. I am amazed that he sees me for me and not for my mental illness.

\*

DENISE PURCELL
Denise was diagnosed with depression, posttraumatic stress
disorder, and dissociative identity disorder in 1995 at age 30

No, not unless I have too. My family knows and people I interact
with know, as well as my therapist and psychiatrist, and people at an
online site. It's okay to vent, and they don't know you, but sometimes
it's just a bunch of triggering going on and nothing helpful. I try to at
least be positive for those who are just finding out, but you only
believe what you want. Sometimes you're stuck in a large black hole
for a long time and can't hear anyone. That's a dangerous place to be.

\*

ERICKA REEVE
Ericka was diagnosed with dissociative identity disorder,
posttraumatic stress disorder, obsessive-compulsive disorder,
depression, anxiety and an eating disorder in 2013 at age 26

This has become something we have been working on over the
last year. We speak more and more on the subject, and write often
about DID, dissociative disorders and mental health in general. This
year, we finally started our own blog, thanks to the support and
encouragement of the wonderful people we've met within the online
mental health community on Twitter.

People in my day-to-day life become more complicated to discuss
these things with. In short yes, we have been working on discussing it
with more people. The trouble seems to be my parts hid and created a
very "normal" persona for myself, in most instances. Not all, but most.
The people we don't speak to much, or haven't and won't likely ever
speak to again, are not of much consequence. My life has always been
compartmentalized in a major way.

\*

LORRAINE SCOTT
Lorraine was diagnosed with non-epilepsy attack disorder
and dissociative identity disorder in 2016 at age 48

When I found out that I had mental illnesses, I was scared as to who I should tell and what, not knowing their reactions toward me and how this knowledge would affect us in the future. The one person I feared telling was my husband of six months. We had been together for seven years and then married, and were just coming up on our six-month anniversary when I got the second diagnosis. I told my husband when I got back from the hospital, and said that the one thing I feared was that he would not want me anymore and would leave me. I now had a mental illness that was in the same group as schizophrenia, which a member of his family lived with, and this was difficult for him.

A few days later, his interest in me became less and eventually he did just what I begged him not to: he told me he didn't want to be with me anymore. I was numb for months, and we've since divorced. I really didn't expect this after being married for only six months, and truly didn't expect this from the man who said he loved me, and vowed to be there through sickness and in health, until death us do part. I don't think anyone can imagine the feelings I went through—it was hell. I went to such a dark place and thought I might never recover, but one day, I saw the light and climbed out of that dark place.

I didn't know how anyone was going to respond but thought my loved ones would be by my side, and my siblings and kids did just that. They all knew my life had been turned upside down, so they weren't just supporting me through illnesses and diagnoses, but also having to move and live in temporary accommodations due to a water leak at our home of twenty-seven years, as well as the abandonment of my husband. It was a lot to deal with, but most of all I felt that now that he had done that, others would also distance themselves from me. My kids and siblings were fine with it. They all said, "We've always thought that about you anyway, so it doesn't make any difference. You're Mom and Lorraine, and that's all that matters." I couldn't have asked for much more support from my loved ones.

I also sat with Sam for a couple of hours questioning him about what I was concerned about, as he had gone through this a year prior to my diagnosis. The questions I asked were:

1. How long did it roughly take him to come to terms with?

2. Did people treat him any different?

3. How did it make him feel as a person?

4. How did it affect him emotionally?

In asking Sam his thoughts on telling others, he personally doesn't feel the need to address this with people. He's not hiding who he is and isn't ashamed of the obstacles he's faced and will face. These obstacles are what shape us into who we are today. He doesn't like to be the center of conversations but would answer any questions to help with awareness and understanding. He used to be fearful of telling others but no longer bears that emotion when approaching the subject after six or seven years of living with the diagnoses.

When it comes to telling other people, I have been very fearful of the questions they may fire at me and the comments they may make. It's only normal to be frightened, but I feared rejection, abandonment, being singled out, bullied, name-calling, and being made to feel different like I have a disease. Some of us are lucky and have understanding families, but some don't.

I've only told a couple of friends who I truly trust. I don't want people looking at me differently, so it's something I keep close to my chest. I know writing my story is a big statement, but I hope that those who read it won't judge or think differently of their sibling, mother, daughter, son, aunty, uncle, friend or the other writers. We are all human, and in addition, we all have specialties.

After my experience when telling my husband, yes, it's made me even more cautious as to who I tell. It's that fear of being rejected, abandoned, singled out, bullied, called and treated like you're crazy or have a contagious disease. That's why it's important to have a good, safe support network. Luckily for some of us, we have a good supportive family who does not judge or see us any different from the person we were named, but some people don't have that. People can be very cruel at times and distance themselves from you when you don't measure up, and they no longer want to associate themselves with someone who has a mental illness.

There is only one word that ignorant people see or hear when you use the term mental illness, and that is "crazy." Then they say, "You don't look like you have a mental illness." Why do people say that? What does a person with mental illness look like? As I said before, we look like every other Joe Blow. This just shows the shallowness of some people. I love it when I'm in a conversation and something about mental illness comes up. I sit and listen to the comments and degrading jokes, and then drop the bombshell about my illnesses, and watch them wanting the floor to open up and swallow them in. Also, they look at you as if your head is going to start spinning and a load of green stuff is about to project from your mouth. "Educate yourselves," is what I say to them.

Due to my illnesses I am currently unable to work, but if I were working, I would have problems telling the people I work with. The last place I worked at, the moment you turned your back, they would spread your business like wildfire and so I couldn't trust any of them with this kind of information. In a way, I'm glad I don't have to face people at work and listen to the whispering behind my back, it would break me again. I also think that if you must disclose this in the workplace, it should be kept personal and go no further, but unfortunately some companies cannot keep track of the ones who leak personal details about others.

*

CARRIE WORTHINGTON
Carrie was diagnosed with depression,
anxiety, and trichotillomania in 2000 at age 41

Over the past ten years, I have spoken more about my depression and anxiety. All my work with NAMI is to help fight against the stigma I experienced with my husband. In my immediate circle, they know about the depression and anxiety. Like I've mentioned earlier, I never speak of the trichotillomania. Ever. Except with my daughter. I share most everything with her and what my current struggle is.

Since my husband's passing and some of the extreme experiences I've had with depression and anxiety, more of my friends have assisted me when I'm having a hard time. I'm still cautious about exactly who I speak to, but it's more acceptable, and a topic of conversation that luckily comes up more often. I speak more about stigma, needed care, needed emergency care, etc. I don't speak in the first-person, but rather use my past experiences, starting with my husband's early diagnosis, to discuss the break down for mental illness care.

CHAPTER FOUR

# Managing with Medication

Bipolar disorder is a scary disease but manageable. I feel blessed that I was able to get the right attention and the right medication to deal with my specific illness. -ERIC MILLEGAN

Medication as treatment for mental illness has come far over the past thirty years, and plays a significant role for the well-being of millions. Like many other diseases, medication doesn't cure mental illness but can significantly improve symptoms enabling many of us to lead rich, fulfilling lives. What medication do you take for your mental illness, and does it help?

\*

ADRIANNE ALLEN-LANG
Adrianne was diagnosed with dissociative
identity disorder in 2015 at age 18

I've tried a number of medications for my illnesses, but only two work, and being a mother to a young child, their sedative affects outweigh the benefits. I'm all for medication use—when used correctly it has amazing benefits. I currently medicate using cannabis and that works well for me.

\*

MORGAN BUTLER
Morgan was diagnosed with depression
and anxiety in 2009 at age 15

I do not take medication, no. I have been offered it before, but counseling and finding coping mechanisms worked for me best. I also personally cannot take melatonin as a sleep-assist because, though it's natural, it pulls me to an awful low in subsequent days.

\*

LYNDA CHELDELIN FELL
Lynda was diagnosed with depression in 2000 at age 35
and posttraumatic stress disorder in 2012 at age 47

I was on and off Prozac for years. It worked very well for me, but eventually its efficacy waned. I'm currently on Zoloft, a serotonin reuptake inhibitor commonly used to treat depression with anxiety.

When a bout of depression begins, I have clear telltale signs including irritability, absence of joy doing things I normally love, and an overwhelming feeling of hopelessness. When those begin to appear and don't resolve within a few days, I know it's not hormonal and will immediately schedule an appointment with my doctor. It's important to be my own advocate. If I needed medication for a bacterial infection, I wouldn't hesitate. I treat my depression similarly.

When Prozac first came on the market in 1986, it carried a huge stigma as a medicine for people looking for a quick fix without first trying fresh air, exercise, and other holistic modalities. Following my hysterectomy when I experienced a bout of depression so severe that it threatened to cripple me, I swallowed my pride, sought treatment, and joined millions of others on Prozac. But at the time, the stigma around taking such a medication kept me living in fear of being judged. Not only was Prozac an excellent medication, its nonaddictive nature and low side effects were bonuses, and general practitioners not skilled in treating mental illness began prescribing it for anyone complaining of depression. The popularity brought huge profits to the pharmaceutical industry, and suddenly the race was on to capitalize on such a virgin market. Although profits drove the pharmaceutical race, nonetheless it paved the way for the development of more medication to treat mental illness. This was progress!

As it is with any disease, medication isn't one size fits all. So while Prozac carried a huge stigma, it is credited with opening the door on a new generation of medication now available to those in need.

Sadly, I just had a discussion this morning with a loved one who is clearly struggling with severe depression but who remains reluctant to take medication. Using myself as a example, I politely explained that depression is an illness and despite our best efforts at holistic treatment, we sometimes still need medical intervention. My argument was to no avail; she remained steadfast that medication was not an option.

We have our work cut out for us, as the stigma continues to run deep in some circles and that is such a shame.

*

SHAUNA COX
Shauna was diagnosed with an
anxiety disorder in 2009 at age 26

When I was first diagnosed with anxiety, my psychologist encouraged me to ask my family doctor to prescribe medication, as he felt this would help complement the cognitive behavioral therapy I was going through. My doctor put me on an antidepressant that also works on anxiety. I took a low dose every day for a month before slowly increasing to an effective dose. I was also given an anxiolytic that I could take when the anxiety was severe, primarily when I was experiencing panic-like attacks.

I found that the anxiolytic helped calm me down, although I could still feel the anxiety in the background of my brain. The antidepressant helped lower the anxiety as well, but had negative side effects that I found difficult. It made my moods too level; I didn't feel any highs anymore. It also made my sex drive dip to the point that I am lucky my husband didn't find comfort elsewhere! The final straw was the amount of weight it caused me to gain in a short amount of time.

I went back to my doctor and asked to be taken off the antidepressant. Because my anxiety wasn't to a point where I felt I could handle it without taking any medication, my doctor switched me to a different antidepressant, rather than taking me completely off everything. I also still had the anxiolytic for the especially bad times. I was on this new medication for about five years with no unpleasant side effects. Throughout this time, I was occasionally still seeing a psychologist and using strategies that I learned in these sessions. When I felt comfortable enough with my progress, I told my doctor that I was ready to try stopping the medication. I've been off the daily antidepressant now for three years, and am happy to say that I am still doing well without it. I do, however, still take an anxiolytic during times I know tend to cause panic like attacks for me.

I believe that early in treatment, it often helps to have medication until you have learned strategies to help cope with symptoms. I also think that there are some instances, and many mental illnesses, in which medication is a lifelong strategy to dealing with illness. There is nothing wrong with needing medication, but the trick is in finding one, or a combination, that works for a particular person with a specific set of symptoms. What works for one person might not work for another. I am lucky to have found a medication that helped me, and given my particular set of circumstances, I am lucky that I was able to get off that medication and still succeed.

*

JANE MCDONALD
Jane was diagnosed with major depressive disorder in 1989,
multiple anxiety disorders in 2001, multiple personality
disorders in 2007, and dissociative identity disorder in 2014

For almost as long as I can remember, I have been on medications for my mental illness. I started out on SSRI antidepressants during the Prozac epidemic of the 1980s when just about everyone was being prescribed the drug for depression. I didn't really think about it much, as it was never a choice for me. I was still young and living with my mother and did as I was told, including taking whatever medication my doctor prescribed me. Eventually, I would try a number of different SSRIs, each with their own costs and benefits. Many worked for a period of time but gradually became ineffective, thus necessitating a change.

Once I was an adult and living on my own, antianxiety meds were added to the mix. I wasn't terribly worried about the stigma because by this time almost everyone was on an antidepressant or antianxiety medication at some point in their lives. However, what did give me trouble were the side effects including nausea, dizziness, lightheadedness, difficulty concentrating, and much more. I continued to take the medications but switched between them frequently.

I never really questioned the need for medication to treat my mental illness. I had studied psychiatry and was well versed in the biochemical nature of many mental illnesses, including depression and anxiety. While I was regularly in some form of therapy, I recognized that talking alone didn't control my symptoms adequately to allow me to function.

It wasn't until I had run through the gamut of antidepressants and was still struggling to find a balance that I started to have difficulties. My psychiatrist at the time began to prescribe me antipsychotic medications which, to me, had a whole other connotation. I wasn't psychotic! I didn't have schizophrenia or any of the "more serious" mental illnesses. I was depressed and anxious. Surely I wasn't psychotic. My psychiatrist assured me that many people who were resistant to SSRIs and other traditional antidepressants showed promising results with antipsychotics, and despite their name, they were actually commonly prescribed for those in my situation. I grudgingly accepted, and started to take an antipsychotic in addition to my antidepressants and antianxiety.

There did come a point, however, where I felt I had taken enough medications. I had been on meds most of my life, and I didn't see my situation or symptoms improving at all. If anything I felt like a zombie, barely feeling any emotion. I was on eleven different psychiatric medications, and against medical advice I decided enough was enough, and stopped a number of them all together. As you might expect, I went into withdrawal: shaking terribly, having huge headaches and nausea, not to mention the psychological states of extreme suicidal ideation and anxiety. I quickly learned that I need to be on at least some medication. But to be on that much medication seemed excessive.

Fortunately, not too long after that, my psychiatrist retired and I was transferred to a new one. This new psychiatrist actually listened to me, heard my concerns, and admitted that I was being highly overmedicated by my previous doctor, and there was no need for it.

Today I am on an antidepressant, antianxiety medication, and an antipsychotic. I am not happy about having to take medications, but I realize it is necessary. If I were diabetic, I wouldn't hesitate to take my insulin, so why should this be any different? I recognize that there is still a lot of stigma associated with taking medication for mental illness, and for some people it is enough for them to get enough exercise, fresh air, and stimulation. However, for many of us it is critical that we deal with the biochemical nature of our mental illnesses, just as we would treat a bacterial infection with antibiotics. We may not like it, but sometimes it is necessary.

\*

AMY OWEN
Amy was diagnosed with ADD and
bipolar disorder in 2014 at age 42

I take medications and they have changed my life. I don't know what I would do without them. They make my life better in so many ways. I make better decisions and I have more confidence in all that I do. My relationship with my kids is the big change. I am grateful for the meds for giving me the ability to be a better mom.

\*

AMBER PILLARS
Amber was diagnosed with
schizophrenia in 2004 at age 24

Yes, I take medicine for my mental illness every night. I feel like my body needs it to keep me balanced. My body chemistry is off and so the antipsychotic and antidepressant medicines are necessary to keep me thriving. I also take antianxiety medicine as needed when things get super stressful in life.

As I shared earlier, it took extreme measures for me to realize how bad I needed to take medicine. I am very careful now to make sure I don't skip a dose. Because any dose that is skipped even for one night, can cause my mood to be slightly off.

I believe it's really hard for people to accept that they may actually need medicine. I know because I used to be one of those people. I am very grateful for the insight and knowledge that I have gained about needing to take medicine. My heart breaks for those people who still haven't come to that conclusion. It needs to come from deep within them for them to understand they need it to keep them balanced. One of the best things you can do for them is pray that they understand how badly they need to take medicine.

*

DENISE PURCELL
Denise was diagnosed with depression, posttraumatic stress disorder, and dissociative identity disorder in 1995 at age 30

I have taken many medications for anxiety and depression, and used cognitive behavior therapy, and EMDR, eye movement desensitization and reprocessing. The only thing that works is the hope of an antidepressant that doesn't cause so many side effects, and maybe hypnotherapy. One day when I'm stronger, I would like to start a DID group but it has to be a very safe place. My emotion is anger at having to deal with this because of others' actions. I will never be cured and that's okay, because I believe it makes me more caring to others, but sometimes I would like to feel wonderful about myself. To not be afraid of going out and losing time, or what I ate or didn't. So, self-acceptance is probably the better of the choices. Good luck on that one though, it's picking apart every thought and emotion you could have about everything and nothing, and rewiring your brain into thinking positive thoughts. Sometimes it's too hard even just getting out of bed,

\*

ERICKA REEVE
Ericka was diagnosed with dissociative identity disorder,
posttraumatic stress disorder, obsessive-compulsive disorder,
depression, anxiety and an eating disorder in 2013 at age 26

I have not ever taken medication. As things progressed in therapy, I voiced some of my concerns regarding this with my therapist. I wanted her to know of dissociative episodes I had that were far more frequent and longer than they had been in nearly six months. I didn't want to go backwards, so if I needed to try antidepressants, antianxiety, and sleep medications, I was very much in agreement with that. I've been sick the majority of my life in some capacity, and have had to take many medications over the years for my physical health problems, which is still true today. I have a tempestuous relationship with medication, but I do know and can logically understand that if it is beneficial, then I should comply.

\*

LORRAINE SCOTT
Lorraine was diagnosed with non-epilepsy attack disorder
and dissociative identity disorder in 2016 at age 48

Although I have been diagnosed with two mental illnesses, I'm not currently taking any medication. Now with my non-epileptic attack disorder, there isn't really any medication, as they are stress related seizures. I was on an antiepileptic drug, which is also used to numb the nerves in your sensory system and therefore is widely used for severe body pain such as spinal and much more. This was great because it also suppressed my seizures but I've had to come off of it, due to severe weight gain and risk of other life threatening illnesses. The seizures are very frequent again, which is the downside of not taking the medication. It took a couple of months to wean off of these, and I am now only on painkillers, which only mask the pain a little bit as all my sensitivity is back. There is medication for dissociative identity disorder, but I don't take any, and don't want to take any, as I don't want to mask it. I want to face it, deal with it, and hopefully find the true Lorraine.

Many, many moons ago, I was told that I had postnatal depression, although I didn't think so. Although I did have a baby a few weeks prior, I was just tired and stressed, I wouldn't have gone as far to say that it was postnatal depression. The doctor put me on antidepressants. I knew that my body didn't like them, and I told the doctor that they didn't sit well with me, but I was told to take them. Within a couple of weeks, I could see a big difference, and it wasn't for the better. My moods became uncontrollable, and I was doing stuff that was totally out of character for me. I had no control and hated the way they were making me feel. My husband at the time distanced himself from me. I contacted the doctor and told him how I was feeling, but he wanted me to stick with them for a couple months. I totally disagreed with this and told him that I was no longer going to take them, and I stopped. After a week, I was getting back to me and could take on the world. I know my body and it really doesn't like antidepressants.

I would say to others however, please do not just stop taking prescribed medication. Always speak to your doctor first and they will work out a weaning-off plan for you that is safe and prevents the severe withdrawal side effects, or they may tell you to stop taking them immediately if it's causing severe side effects. Either way, speak to your doctor first. My views on medication is as such:

PROS:

- There are two ways to treat mental illness: one is therapy and the other is medication. The medication can help alongside the therapy, to help you feel better faster.

- Medication can treat some symptoms that may not be able to be treated or cured with therapy.

- Also, using medication could help to suppress some of the symptoms enabling you to do day-to-day jobs, socialize, and work more effectively. It could help to get you back to some form of normality.

CONS:

- I don't like needing pills to be happy.

- I don't want to be known as someone who needs antidepressants and be labeled for this.

- Taking medication is sometimes seen as being weak and the "easy way out."

- I am fearful of taking them and becoming dependent or addicted and needing them for the rest of my life.

- A fear of needing something stronger and seeking other types of drugs.

- A fear of feeling better and being weaned off the medication but weeks after having a relapse.

- Medication doesn't cure mental illnesses, it just suppresses it.

- The side effects of taking medication and other illnesses they may cause.

- It has been said that some antidepressants can make you feel more depressed or even suicidal.

- When I took them for a very short period many years ago, they didn't seem to make much difference, other than making me aggressive, but this isn't the case for all.

- I fear the thought of false happiness, which turns into depression again once you are no longer taking the medication.

Other people I have spoken with said the following about taking medication:

- One strongly disagrees with taking medication, but that is regarding himself; it works for some people, but not all, and everyone's body reacts to it differently.

- One believes that mental illness is controllable without the need for medication. This however, is dependent upon one's mental willingness, mindfulness and awareness (remember, this is just an opinion).

- On taking medication in the past, it subdued his consciousness and he spent most of his time sleeping and wanted to do nothing more. He wasn't aware of his surroundings and felt like his mind was locked in a cage. This caused him to become very angry and suicidal. He had no energy to redirect these emotions as the medication had suppressed that. They made him feel worse emotionally and safe physiologically.

Ways in which to redirect your thoughts and to help you manage your mental illness:

- Put your thoughts into an image.

- Create something like a painting, drawing, sculpture, or anything that you enjoy, really.

- Write your thoughts and feelings down. Keep a diary, journal, a daily log, or even write a poem.

- Find a hobby like sewing, crafts, photography, or writing. This will keep your mind active and happy achievement emotions will flow. Frustration may play a role at some points, but that will be because something isn't going right.

*

CARRIE WORTHINGTON
Carrie was diagnosed with depression,
anxiety, and trichotillomania in 2000 at age 41

I went through a horrible Paxil withdrawal where I was psychotic and couldn't work for over six weeks. One year after my husband passed away, my therapist suggested that I go on antidepressants. I had one or two suicidal thoughts as well when in the midst of several panic attacks. It took me about a year until I agreed I wasn't functioning as I should. I have always talked about mental illness being an illness where medicine can and should help, yet here I was too proud to take medication.

I went to the same psychiatrist who saw my husband and kids. I saw him every few weeks until we found a good antidepressant dose.

I would only take the antidepressant I had been on previously because I was so concerned about the side effects. The doctor kept trying to get me to take Paxil. Upon hearing how against it I was, he tried to get me to take Prozac. I refused this also because it's a lighter version of Paxil, and I'll never take an SSRI. We settled on Xanax and I managed to find a good medication routine with Xanax and Wellbutrin.

With medicines, exercise, and therapy, I am in a very good place right now. I no longer see a psychiatrist for my med management because he keeps pushing me to take Prozac. I do see my general practitioner, whom I've known for seventeen years. He respects my wishes, thoughts, and opinions about Prozac, asks the right questions, and will discuss medication management instead of telling me what is going to happen. From being part of the mental illness world for so long, I know about meds and side effects, and I certainly know what I need. I like going to a doctor who knows me. Psychiatrists are overbooked, the visits are too short, and the number of available psychiatrists is declining. I'm very interested in a law that would let psychologists manage medication. I would feel comfortable with this. If I spoke to someone every week, every other week or even every month, I would assume they would notice changes in behavior, or no changes for that matter. I believe this would be a good relationship for taking meds.

I was very resistant about going back on medication but it does help. In fact, I have been very stable lately and I have found other ways to avoid more medications. Exercise is so wonderful for my brain. I have found mindfulness eases the anxiety a great deal. I do wish to be med free someday.

*

CHAPTER FIVE

# Facing Social Barriers

> Many people believe that introversion is about being antisocial, and that's really a misperception. Because actually it's just that introverts are differently social. So they would prefer to have a glass of wine with a close friend as opposed to going to a loud party full of strangers. -SUSAN CAIN

The stigma associated with mental illness creates huge barriers for many, and it has been argued that people with a mental illness are among the most excluded in society. One social assumption is that those who live with mental illness are predisposed to violence. Racism, poverty, and homelessness are also commonly associated with mental illness. These perceptions create an invisible barrier that make it difficult to find social support. In what ways has your mental illness impacted your social life?

*

ADRIANNE ALLEN-LANG
Adrianne was diagnosed with dissociative
identity disorder in 2015 at age 18

My mental illness has impacted my social life dramatically. I rarely go out and when I do, it isn't for long. I find it extremely difficult to create and maintain friendships and relationships due to my fluctuating mood and personalities. Interacting with people on a social level is very draining and anxiety-inducing for me. I don't like crowds, and some of my alters have their own fears about being in public, which is overwhelming. I find though, it's more myself that stops my social life. Others are accommodating to begin with, but I push them away most of the time to protect myself.

*

MORGAN BUTLER
Morgan was diagnosed with depression
and anxiety in 2009 at age 15

Mental illness has definitely impacted the way that I choose my social interactions and scheduling, but an excellent way to combat depression is to counteract it with social interactions. Ironic, huh? Anxiety makes this difficult at times, and on days when it's really flaring up, I bail on my plans. This is usually due to complete overthinking—a result of anxiety—and some sort of excuse or worry in my head blows up, and I end up backing out. This has resulted in extreme FOMO (Fear Of Missing Out), and is something I'm currently still combating.

*

LYNDA CHELDELIN FELL
Lynda was diagnosed with depression in 2000 at age 35
and posttraumatic stress disorder in 2012 at age 47

Prior to losing my daughter and my husband's stroke, I equated social activities with one's popularity and worth because that's how I was raised. Forced to create a very different life out of the ashes of my former life, and being a bereaved mother leaving many to feel awkward around me, I find I'm happiest making a difference in the world by working magic from behind the curtain. At times, my work requires me to travel, host this or that, take the stage or be in front of the camera, or what have you. I compartmentalize very well, so I can be on queue at the drop of a hat. But because my social battery drains quickly, I'm careful to spend my energy on fulfilling endeavors and be mindful of the social gatherings I choose to attend.

*

SHAUNA COX
Shauna was diagnosed with an
anxiety disorder in 2009 at age 26

I think because I have tended to avoid social interactions that involve big groups of people, and I have said no to such invitations so many times, the invitations are coming fewer and farther between. Even my husband doesn't ask me to come along with him as often, and I'm sure it's because nine times out of ten, when he invites me along, he gets the familiar, "No, you go ahead without me." He at least knows, that a big part of why I say no to going along to parties or get-togethers is because of the anxiety that I feel at such events. My friends, while they know that I have an anxiety disorder, don't know or understand just how uncomfortable I am in big groups. They do know, however, that if they ask me to go with them to events, I will likely say no, and so a lot of them have stopped asking.

It makes me sad to know that because of the anxiety, I have missed out on going to places or events that probably would have ended up being fun. I tend to be incredibly anxious at the idea of going, and still anxious while there, but when looking back on my experience I realize that I had a good time and that it was worth going out. Perhaps if more of my friends understood what it is I go through when invited, and the anxiety I feel when at social events, they would continue to invite me and try to support me more during the event. While I struggle with feeling like I need to tackle my anxiety on my own and not put it on other people, I know that sometimes I need help and support, and what better source of support than from one's friends and loved ones?

\*

JANE MCDONALD
Jane was diagnosed with major depressive disorder in 1989, multiple anxiety disorders in 2001, multiple personality disorders in 2007, and dissociative identity disorder in 2014

Truth be told I have never had much of a "social life." I've always been extremely shy and very introverted. I prefer time by myself. However, I have made efforts to make friends and have had limited success. This was relatively easier for me when I was younger, but that changed in the sixth grade. At that point, even my best friends rejected me along with all my other classmates, and I was left alone. I cannot say for sure if I was rejected because of my mental illness, but I suspect that was the case. I had always been a very serious, contemplative person and often felt sad. I firmly believe that this was the reason that I never received many social invitations, and was not invited to birthday parties or sleepovers much. The few invitations that I did receive all ended come the sixth grade. This only made me even more introverted and deepened my sadness which, I am sure, resulted in less and less of a social life and eliminated almost all social invitations.

I think people had a hard time relating to me. Most kids are pretty happy and carefree. I was never like this. I was unhappy at home and this reflected in how I was at school.

As an adult, I still had very few friends. I made some in university and we did hang out at times, but I still spent the vast majority of my time alone. At this time, it wasn't so much that my friends were uncomfortable around me. They understood depression and anxiety and never judged me for it. However, I myself carried a great fear of developing friendships based on my experiences of rejection and abandonment in elementary school. I feared that friends would learn the "truth" about me, about my mental illness, and would judge me and find that I wasn't someone they wanted to be around. My natural introversion combined with my fear of social rejection has meant that I lead a largely solitary life with only a few close friends.

The other difficulty with making friends, or indeed with any relationship, stems from my borderline personality disorder. People with this disorder tend to idolize people they are in relationships with, and when even the smallest argument occurs, they then completely devalue and reject the friend. A common expression for those of us with borderline personality disorder is, "I hate you, don't leave me." I know I can become clingy with new friends and be very close to them one minute and then push them away the next. This isn't always easy to tolerate in a friendship.

Everything is black and white for me. The friend is the best thing one minute, and then a horrible person the next. I have tried very hard to change this but it isn't easy to override one's basic personality traits. As a result, I find it best to avoid relationships most of the time. Every now and then I make a close friend but I consciously try to spend as little time with them as possible because I don't want to overwhelm them, become dependent or clingy, or find one thing I dislike and have it distort my entire perception of the person.

\*

AMY OWEN
Amy was diagnosed with ADD and
bipolar disorder in 2014 at age 42

I do not go to many events because I get too nervous. I'm not good in crowds. I avoid groups with everyone. I don't get asked as much and if I do, they usually say, "Just try to come." But I most likely will not make it. Most of the people do not understand that it's not them, and can't understand why my disorder makes it hard for me to go.

\*

AMBER PILLARS
Amber was diagnosed with
schizophrenia in 2004 at age 24

During the onset of my schizophrenia, my social interactions changed drastically. I had gone from a friendly, bubbly, outgoing person to a scared, untrusting, introverted person. I had minimal contact with people because I couldn't communicate what was going on inside of me to hardly anyone. I hated being in large crowds of people. It was just too much for me.

After I was released from the hospital and taking my medicine, parts of my friendly, bubbly, outgoing personality slowly started to emerge again. My best friend from college, Brooke, had introduced me to a group of young adults from her church. I started hanging out with them. We hung out on weekends, played sand volleyball, enjoyed sharing our faith in bible studies, and traveled out of town for trips to Chicago and skiing in Colorado. I began to build some strong friendships that are still thriving today (a decade later). I have since moved to different places in the Midwest. In each place I moved, I developed some great friendships and many acquaintance friendships.

Dating is another story. It is very difficult to know the right time to share about my mental illness, and how much to share, with the guy. I want the guy to know me for me, and I want to be able to share more about my past, present, and future. How do I share with a guy that I want to have my own kids, but I'm not entirely sure it's possible? It is not recommended to get pregnant while taking the antidepressant and antipsychotic medicines that I take. The pregnancy categories are a C or D. And I know I *need* my medicine to keep me balanced. I struggle with this so much, because I really do want to have my own kids. So, how do you say this to a guy who could potentially be a boyfriend, fiancée, or husband? But I know that the guy who loves me enough will be the one who sticks around.

*

DENISE PURCELL
Denise was diagnosed with depression, posttraumatic stress
disorder, and dissociative identity disorder in 1995 at age 30

It's impacted my life because I'm aware of my mental illness. I go to functions with a plan. If I become overwhelmed with too many people or questions, I will exit. I know where they are all located. If I go out, I will give myself an hour and then check in and see if I'm okay with staying longer. If anyone wants to visit, I have to know in advance so I can be prepared. I don't do spontaneous visits very well. I feel violated and angry. I always need to compose myself and put on my mask to face the world. That is not very often. Grocery shopping, and appointments are pretty much the only things I do unless I'm feeling a high day and my depression is at a low. Sometimes, going somewhere where no one knows me allows me to feel more free. They don't know me, I don't know them, so if something happens I don't have to see them in my everyday life. In my everyday life, I am very good at putting on an act, making sure everyone is happy and taken care of. It is very exhausting. A lot of times, I wish I could just say how I really feel and pull the covers over my head. That is not acceptable.

*

ERICKA REEVE
Ericka was diagnosed with dissociative identity disorder, posttraumatic stress disorder, obsessive-compulsive disorder, depression, anxiety and an eating disorder in 2013 at age 26

I've found that in some instances, yes, I do receive less invitations. But that has more so to do with who the person is and not because of the anxiety or depression. Those two things are what people know more about, and that is still very minimal. Mental illness has always had an impact on my social life. I am not very social, nor do I have much desire to be most days. There are a select few people I interact with and even fewer who bring me some semblance of positivity when we do communicate. So in short, it greatly impacts my life but not in the way you think. It is because of my DID that I have a social life. It would likely be completely nonexistent if it weren't for Jynx.

*

LORRAINE SCOTT
Lorraine was diagnosed with non-epilepsy attack disorder and dissociative identity disorder in 2016 at age 48

I have tried to keep my social life as active as my illnesses will allow. I have been open about my seizures, and most of my family and relatives know about them, as do a few of my friends. My other illness I have kept to a handful of people other than my immediate family and very close friends (my safe network). I only divulge that information if necessary, but I don't need to at the moment because it isn't a risk to others or me, so there doesn't seem to be any need at present. Most of them don't even look at it as being a mental health problem, and if they do, they've said nothing to me.

The seizures have a profound impact on me and others who are there to witness them, so we all focus on them, to be honest. These are what has an impact on my whole life. When I have a seizure or blackout, we never know how or who I will be when I come around. I can feel vulnerable, upset, embarrassed, confused, aggressive and have memory loss. On top of that, I may have switched persons, too, and child Lorraine will appear or teenage Lorraine. Once I'm safe and have slept it off, one of my others will come back and take the forefront. Five-year-old Lorraine mainly appears after a seizure. My seizures started when I was a toddler and have been there ever since in some shape or form. Those around me know what to do if I have a seizure while with them. If I'm going out with a friend who has not yet experienced one, I will brief them on what to do before we go out.

Family and friends all treat me the same and know what my limits are. I have found that since I haven't been driving and out and about as much, it's amazing the people who don't bother with you anymore. At first I thought it was just me being sensitive, but it isn't so. People see you as ill and incapable, and that's it. When I go out, I have to have a chaperone or caregiver with me so I have someone I trust to deal with me when I have a seizure or blackout.

At first, it bothered me that people stopped contacting me or never bothered with me anymore, but now I don't care and it doesn't get to me. I know the people who contact me daily and weekly are all genuine and do genuinely care, and I appreciate all that they do to help me feel valued and loved. I've learned to just get on with things as always, and as long as my kids and grandkids are okay, then I'm happy. I've always been there for others and always will be, no matter what illnesses I have. If I can help, I will. If I can't, then I give advice.

I still get invitations, even though at one point I couldn't attend functions for a few years. Family and friends still send invites to me, just in case I'm having a good day and can attend. I have a two-hour window when I go out before the changes begin and the main seizure or blackout will happen. I have absent seizures all the time, although these are less noticeable to some, but I know I've had them and my kids know when I'm having them as well.

If I want to go on a shopping trip and it's a long distance, then I will book a hotel. This helps give me somewhere to rest and a safe place away from the public if a seizure is coming on. After a seizure, I will be out for hours, sometimes well over eight hours, so it's best to get me to a bed so I can rest and recover. We also do this if we are going to functions out of town, that way I can be attended to immediately and it's less stress on the driver, who might feel that he or she has to speed to get me home quicker.

I do, however, have a problem with parties. I try to avoid them because of the flashing lights, noise level of the music, and all the conversations which sound like just lots of noise. These are all triggers and I won't last two hours, that's for sure. I do try and attend some, but I've ended up in the car in the carpark surrounded by people within the first hour. It doesn't matter where I'm going. A seizure can start from the moment the car is in motion, so we never know what state I'm going to be in by the time I get to my destination.

It saddens me to see that I, a party girl who loved music and dancing the night away, now can't stand long enough to dance because the flashing lights and loudness triggers my seizures. I will sit there sadly watching everyone do what I once could, wishing that I could dance to just one song, but the pain in my spine won't let that happen. I pray that one day I will get to dance again and enjoy the one thing that brought me fulfillment. The thing that allowed me to drift into the world of music, singing as if I'm the only person there embracing, feeling, and floating away to the song with my face glowing wide with a smile, showing how happy I was every time I danced.

So, this is the impact that my illnesses have on my social life and getting out and about. I'm glad that others do try to include me in their plans, and I do my best to fulfill their expectations by attending. It may be ten minutes or two hours that I'm there, but they're happy just to see me there. I'm lucky, as I know some people would be secluded because of their illnesses.

*

CARRIE WORTHINGTON
Carrie was diagnosed with depression,
anxiety, and trichotillomania in 2000 at age 41

My mental illness has not really had any effect on my social life as far as being invited to things. My social circle is completely accepting to my diagnosis, I think in part, because the dealing with grief has been a large part of the roller coaster that was the last five years. I believe in today's world, depression and anxiety are much more acceptable. I think when I'm not feeling well, I can stay home and hide, most of the time. It is not like fifteen or twenty years ago when my husband, who had bipolar and was sometimes not acting right, was shunned from many of our circles and we lost a few friends and family members. When this happened to us, I'm not sure how much he was aware of how people just stopped coming by, calling, inviting, but I knew his illness was not who he was. After the initial shock of being shunned, I felt like I really didn't want those people in my life if they were so close-minded or ignorant about mental illness (which, back then, was probably eighty percent of the population). It wasn't discussed, recognized, or I guess acceptable at the time. For me now, things are so different and being through what I did with my husband's passing, I make sure those I want to be with are ones who accept me (and the understanding of mental illness). If they don't, it doesn't matter, I wouldn't want to be around them.

*

# CHAPTER SIX

# understanding Avoidance

At some point, life starts to pass you by and becomes about avoidance. I want to stay clear from that situation, because I don't like that. - DANIEL CRAIG

Avoiding social interaction or certain social settings is commonly thought of as a hallmark for mental illness as a whole. While some consider it a pitfall, others find social avoidance or isolation a welcome respite from judgment and societal standards that leave us feeling inadequate. In the end, we must do what feels best for our mental needs at the moment. Do you avoid certain social settings or social interactions?

\*

ADRIANNE ALLEN-LANG
Adrianne was diagnosed with dissociative
identity disorder in 2015 at age 18

No, I just get up and get on with it. You just get to the stage where it needs to be done, and you just have to choke back the tears while pushing the grocery cart around and try not to dissociate or run into someone. I avoid most recreational social events and settings due to this, but regular things like shopping, appointments, and school, I just suck it up and get on it with. If it gets really bad, one of my alters will periodically take over.

*

MORGAN BUTLER
Morgan was diagnosed with depression
and anxiety in 2009 at age 15

I find myself commonly avoiding settings where I don't know the majority of the people attending. For example, I was invited to a BBQ where I would know only two of the attendees, and I had a hard time leaving the house to do that. Luckily, a friend called and said they wanted to pick me up to go, so she convinced me. Sometimes I have really bad anxiety about driving. I'm not sure where this comes from, but when I get home from work (driving to and from work has its own set of triggers for me), I just want to sit on the couch with my dog, no matter how desperately I need groceries. I've gotten around to going about every three weeks now, and I'm slowly working on going more often.

*

LYNDA CHELDELIN FELL
Lynda was diagnosed with depression in 2000 at age 35
and posttraumatic stress disorder in 2012 at age 47

I have a tendency to not buy what others deem a pitfall. If social isolation or avoiding certain social settings is better for me in that moment, then I honor my emotional needs. But my mental illness, the depression and PTSD, don't prevent me from attending social settings.

Prior to our daughter's accident, I was very social. I served on many boards and volunteered many hours over decades. But losing a child marred me; I found myself very different from normal people. They suddenly found it awkward to be around me, and there was nothing I could do to ease their discomfort. I was just so very broken; I had nothing left to give. It was much easier to hibernate than to spin my wheels trying to narrow the gap that now lay between me and society. I suppose this is when I began to find comfort by isolating myself, protecting everyone else from the smile of a brokenhearted mother. Now it's my comfort zone.

I strongly dislike shopping. Whether it be for groceries, running errands, or clothes shopping, I've never enjoyed it and this makes me somewhat of an anomaly in my family. I cope with errands, appointments, and groceries by planning my trips as efficiently as possible. And I treat myself to whatever Starbucks frappuccino is in season while running errands. If I have to shop for a new outfit, I'm in and out quickly. I'm not a browser, and I can often tell within a few minutes whether I'll buy something or leave empty handed. Thank goodness for Amazon; it's how I do all my Christmas shopping now: from my recliner using my iPad!

*

SHAUNA COX
Shauna was diagnosed with an
anxiety disorder in 2009 at age 26

Shortly before receiving my diagnosis, my anxiety was probably eight out of ten, if a ranking existed. I avoided most settings that involved social interaction, especially those that involved standing in lines where I felt like escape would be impossible, difficult, or embarrassing. If I had to go shopping, for example, I would make sure my husband came with me so that if I started to feel panicky, I could make a quick escape outside, knowing that he was still in there taking care of business. If I had a doctor's or dentist's appointment, I would make sure to schedule myself first or last so that my time there would be as short as possible, and I would often take an anxiolytic ahead of time to calm my nerves. I still do the same when traveling by plane and shopping in a big mall, as I know that the crowds and line-ups tend to trigger an anxiety attack.

Today, I have progressed to the point where I can go shopping without dragging my husband along, although I still avoid big trips on my own. I can also go to a mall without taking medication beforehand. I do, however, still take an antianxiety medication for flying, as the line-up into the plane is one thing that never fails to make me anxious! I'm also good now at distracting myself from the anxiety that would otherwise be building up inside of me. I concentrate my mind on my breathing, and on feeling the tips of my toes all the way up to the top of my head as slowly as possible. Or, I'll empty my mind completely, and focus my gaze on something in front of me, like a magazine in a grocery aisle.

The one social situation that I still find incredibly difficult to handle, and that I try to avoid at all costs, are parties or big social gatherings where I don't know many people. My husband told me recently that some of his friends were convinced that he had made me up; they were sure that I didn't really exist because I never come along with him to any of the parties he attends. That is something that I have struggled with since I was young. I feel socially awkward in large groups, and I find myself overanalyzing every little thing that I say or do. I feel like everyone is looking at me or judging me. I know that they aren't, but even knowing that, it's a hard feeling to shake. When I'm at a party, I tend to glue myself to my husband because I can't bear to be by myself, and I'm too anxious to go up to a group of people I don't know well and join in on the conversation. I tend to sit on the sidelines and observe, trying to be invisible. All the while, I'm thinking inside how I wish I could be like everyone else. I wish I could mingle, have fun, relax. But my heart is racing, my palms get sweaty, I'm shaking inside, and I'm thinking, thinking, thinking...

There are times when I've forced myself to go along with my husband, but I make him promise ahead of time that he will stay with me. I know that's not fair to him, because there are times when he wants to go off with the guys and expects that I'll stay with the girls. Most of the time, it actually goes well and the girls try to include me as much as possible. But I still can't shake the anxious feelings I have when he's not there. He's my safety net, and it's hard to jump into the fun without it.

*

JANE MCDONALD
Jane was diagnosed with major depressive disorder in 1989,
multiple anxiety disorders in 2001, multiple personality
disorders in 2007, and dissociative identity disorder in 2014

I have always been a very introverted person and have never gone out of my way to seek out social situations, however it wasn't until I was ten years old that I began to purposely avoid them. It was at this age that all of my classmates, including those I had identified as friends, decided to outright reject me, ridicule me at every opportunity, and to torment and tease me every day at school. On a good day, I was ignored. Those were rare though. Most days I was made fun of, insulted, even physically assaulted by the people I had once called my friends. As a result, I developed an intense fear of social situations. I no longer felt safe in the company of others. I firmly believe that this was the beginning of my social anxiety disorder, something which continues to plague me to this day.

I avoid meeting people as much as possible because there is always a deep-seated fear that they will either reject me outright or, worse, pretend to befriend me only to turn around and ridicule me later or abandon me all together.

I tend to avoid almost any situation that involves a lot of people, particularly when those people are strangers. This includes anything from taking public transit, to grocery shopping, to visiting libraries, to accessing social services, and more. Essentially, I stay inside my apartment most of the time and mind my own business. There are certain steps that I take when I am required to go out in public but there is always a great deal of anxiety that remains, despite the coping techniques I use. I tend to use things like music, games on my cell phone, books to read, and other things to distract me when I am on public transit. When grocery shopping, I tend to go with a "safe" person who understands that I suffer panic attacks, is familiar with the signs of when one is coming on, and knows what to do (basically, to get me out of there as soon as possible). I also carry antianxiety medication with me that I take only if I absolutely have to. Overall, this social anxiety makes daily living rather difficult.

Part of the reason for my avoidance of social situations is a fear of being judged, ridiculed, tormented, teased, or otherwise made to feel inadequate by others. This can be something they say to me, or even something as simple as the wrong "look," which makes me paranoid that they think I am a horrible person. I know that a large part of this social anxiety is because of the social rejection I experienced as a child. It is also common for people with my particular personality disorders, particularly avoidant and borderline personality disorders, to fear the worst of social interactions and, thus, to avoid them.

Another concern has to do with my dissociative identity disorder. There is a great fear that another personality will emerge when I am in a social situation and that they may act, speak, think, or otherwise do something inappropriate or even dangerous. I have "woken up" standing in the middle of an aisle at the grocery store with people staring at me and I had no recollection of how I got there or what I was doing. I have also woken up standing in the middle of a street with cars honking at me. On both occasions, I felt absolutely humiliated. Unfortunately, I often have very little awareness and no control over what personality will emerge at what time or for how long, let alone what they will say or do. This increases my already exaggerated fear of being in public or social situations.

I do wish at times that I was more social, that I felt comfortable making friends. Unfortunately the reality is that I do not, I am not there yet. I hope that with therapy and the right medications, I can learn techniques to manage my anxiety and gain some semblance of a normal social life.

*

AMY OWEN<br>Amy was diagnosed with ADD and<br>bipolar disorder in 2014 at age 42

Yes. I don't go to the lunch room at work. I stay in my classroom and eat, or get things done. I avoid going to the store and I ask others to go because I feel like people are staring at me and judging me. I ask other people to take my kids to their friend's so I don't have to talk to the parents. I feel "less" than them, and that stresses me out. I don't go to therapy because talking about my issues makes me feel like I'm not a good person. I hate shopping because I might see someone I know and have to talk to them. That is very hard because my girls miss out on this time with me, and that kills me. I just want to be at home all the time.

*

DENISE PURCELL

Denise was diagnosed with depression, posttraumatic stress disorder, and dissociative identity disorder in 1995 at age 30

Grocery shopping, I just stick to myself. Sometimes I find myself doing something I'm embarrassed about, so I will strike up a small conversation with whomever might have seen it. I try to laugh it off until I can leave and breakdown and cry.

Doctor appointments are easy, they know me. The therapist and even my primary physicians know why I'm there and what I have. With the HIPPA laws in effect, it makes it easier to be okay. Although I have had someone tell people I was in the hospital because of my seizures. That got back to the children's school and they felt they had to defend me. I took matters to the hospital and made a formal complaint. I can tell if it's a good day or not. If I'm very anxious and wary of driving, I won't, or will see if my daughter is going out and about.

\*

ERICKA REEVE

Ericka was diagnosed with dissociative identity disorder,
posttraumatic stress disorder, obsessive-compulsive disorder,
depression, anxiety and an eating disorder in 2013 at age 26

Yes, all of them for the most part. An example would be: the
Super Bowl is tomorrow; big, big American football game for those
unfamiliar. Our friends (ours and my husband's) have invited us over
again and I don't have much desire to go. I prefer quiet or noise(s) I
can control. A group of loud people watching football on television
does not fall under this controlled noise heading.

We will be grocery shopping today, and with the help of some of
my parts we can now do this with ease. Through our years in therapy,
this has drastically changed for the better. Doctor appointments can
become very tricky though, depending upon the type of doctor and
reasons for the visit.

\*

LORRAINE SCOTT

Lorraine was diagnosed with non-epilepsy attack disorder
and dissociative identity disorder in 2016 at age 48

For years, I did avoid certain settings but as we learned more
about my seizures, time frames, and triggers, we worked out how to
deal with them and what plans need to be put in place for me to get
out and about, shopping, appointments, and attending functions.
Caregiver, wheelchair, medication, and a hotel are key factors in
enabling this to happen.

At first, I would avoid any social situation and I wouldn't leave
the house except for appointments and to see my kids and grandkids.

I hated going anywhere where there would be lots of people like pubs, bars, restaurants, shopping, and parties. I feared the fact that if I had a seizure, people would be staring at me, and not knowing how or who I was when I came around was embarrassing for me. I didn't want anyone to see that, apart from those in my home. I didn't even like to go and visit people in their homes, because I was so scared of them seeing what happens with me. I didn't trust anyone not to go and laugh about me, and tell other people how bad they saw me. I have always been very OCD about my appearance, and would never let anyone see me without makeup. You can all imagine how fearful I was if anyone saw me having a seizure.

Most of the scenes I avoided were also because of noise levels and flashing lights. I couldn't even go to the cinema. From age twelve to forty-three, I went to the cinemas and could never understand why I conked out half hour after the movie started. I never thought anything of it because I never educated myself about seizures. I spent my youth avoiding the topic of seizures as this would prevent me from going on school trips, joining in on some activities, and other outings. I would lie about it so I could join in. When going somewhere, I make sure I'm well rested prior and that all plans have been put into place, so whoever is with me knows what to do.

I struggle with daily routines, and from one minute to the next, I don't know when I'm going to have a seizure and I may only have a few seconds or warning signs, which is too late by then. The other problem is that, depending on the situation, I may have switched personalities. I don't like being in situations where people are angry or aggressive, and this will trigger a switch, and I will go into verbal aggressive mode to protect myself. I wouldn't hurt anyone physically, it would be verbal. Another trigger of this is bullying, so I'm very careful of where I am and if I sense anything, I will ask to be taken home because although I may switch, the stress will also trigger a seizure or blackout, and God knows what may have happened. So, I do the right thing and leave before anything happens.

When I'm doing group therapy sessions, I find that sometimes things may be said that are triggers to others, and I was in a setting once where I was very scared of the behavior of another member. I really didn't want to go back because seeing that seemed to pull me back down again, and at the time I had just come out of a very deep, dark place and I didn't want to go back there again. I felt that these sessions were going to put me back in that dark place. I also avoid some of the social groups I'm in, because it's upsetting when some are being horrible. I will sit back and watch for a while, and then dip my finger in. If it gets bit, then I'll withdraw from the group. I know that I would never say anything to hurt or upset others, but people don't really know you in these social groups. I'll also watch how people are speaking, and if it's something that is depressing, again I will withdraw from the group because I'm trying to get better and not everyone can deal with someone else's traumas. Don't get me wrong, I do feel for all those who have endured traumas in their lives, but sometimes it's too close to home and brings your own experiences to the forefront. What I'm trying to say is if you're on a low, you don't want to feel lower, because that could push you to another level that you may not be able to, or be strong enough to come back from.

The other thing I avoid is speaking on the phone for more than ten minutes, as this will trigger a conk out followed by a seizure. With knowing this, when I'm on the phone if it's someone who I know will keep me on there for some time, I will tell them at the beginning of the call that I will conk out and have a seizure if I'm on the phone any longer than ten minutes, so be prepared as it will go silent or you may hear me having a seizure. It's not nice as this as happened numerous times and scared the person on the other end, so I warn people now when I answer my phone.

*

CARRIE WORTHINGTON
Carrie was diagnosed with depression,
anxiety, and trichotillomania in 2000 at age 41

Since I have become a widow, going into large groups not knowing if I will be the only single one, causes me to worry all the time. Even when it is close friends, I tend to ask questions, I need to know who will be there because I want to avoid the feeling I get when it is all couples and me. I will not go to some things if that is the case, even though I know everyone at the gathering. It is something that I have been sensitive about and it does cause some anxiety. How I handle routine errands does not cause me any anxiety about the social interaction, but I had a horrible time right after my husband passed away. He was a stay-at-home dad, and for twenty-three years did everything for our home and family like shopping, errands, cooking, and cleaning. After he died, I could not face doing some of the things that needed to be done. My daughter had this covered for the first year, as I was literally incapable of some of the basic things. I have been president of nonprofit boards, manager of many people, spoken in front of groups, but I was immobilized to go to the grocery store, fill the car with gas (yes, he did that for me too), and many other things including taking the garbage cans to the curb. I had to set a reminder on my phone when it was garbage day. At the time of his death, I was incredibly well both mentally and physically. I had gone through bariatric surgery and as the pounds fell off, I became more and more in control of my thoughts. I had no anxiety, and was getting my life back in order. When he passed away, I fell into a darkness like I've never known. So doing routine errands didn't provoke anxiety because I couldn't or had never done them, rather, they were my reminder that he was gone. I would get angry while at the grocery store I hadn't ever been in. One of my dearest friends received many calls from me because I would be frustrated and then anxious when I couldn't find an item I needed and couldn't figure out which aisle it was in. I would walk through the aisles so sad that it took much longer than it should. A lot of the times I sat home, anxious that I had to face it. It would be days overdue before I could catch my breath and face the fear and anxiety.

I'm no longer sad or angry when I shop. Very few people who know me are actually aware how hard and painful this was for me. Time has made it a routine, and it is no longer an issue. Once in a while, when something comes along, like taking the dog to the vet, which I had my daughter do the last few times, it might cause anxiety and hesitation until I know I just have to do it. I've learned that usually it is never as bad as imagined, and is something I can get through very easily.

*

Every rainbow begins with rain.
-UNKNOWN

*

# CHAPTER SEVEN

# Being in Public

Success depends upon previous preparation, and
without such preparation there is sure to be failure.
-CONFUCIUS

For those who prefer solitude, sometimes we just can't avoid having
to go out in public. Strategies crafted in advance can help ensure a
successful outing that minimizes triggers and pitfalls. What steps do
you take beforehand to prepare yourself? What steps do you take
during outings to ensure your comfort?

*

ADRIANNE ALLEN-LANG
Adrianne was diagnosed with dissociative
identity disorder in 2015 at age 18

If I'm in a situation where I'm not coping and can't remove myself
from the situation, one of my alters usually takes over until the
situation has ceased. I try to remember my grounding and meditation
techniques. Breathing, focusing away from my emotion, listening to
music or focusing on my phone if I'm waiting somewhere helps a lot.

*

MORGAN BUTLER
Morgan was diagnosed with depression
and anxiety in 2009 at age 15

Making sure to call a friend or my aunt about what I'm about to do generally helps. Going to Sounders games is a normal thing for me now and I no longer experience anxiety with going there alone. Most everywhere else though, I try and find company.

*

LYNDA CHELDELIN FELL
Lynda was diagnosed with depression in 2000 at age 35
and posttraumatic stress disorder in 2012 at age 47

I use time limits a lot. I tell myself that I'll attend this or that, and leave within ninety minutes or two hours, or whatever. This not only helps me to plan, it gives me an out. It sounds very calculating, and I don't mean for it to. I just enjoy my work very much, and am most comfortable immersed in my work at my desk. So when involved in a social engagement or activity, if I stay too long I begin to worry about work piling up. Planning ahead and setting timelines reduces the fray.

*

SHAUNA COX
Shauna was diagnosed with an
anxiety disorder in 2009 at age 26

As much as going to a party triggers anxiety in me, I know that my husband is incredibly social and so sometimes I will force myself to attend a party with him. I do usually end up having fun in hindsight, and one of the strategies I have used, as bad as it might be to say, is to have a bit of alcohol. It helps loosen me up a bit and gets me out of my own head so that I can forget some of the anxiety and have fun. If I can't drink, an antianxiety pill before going to a party can help as well. I also try and remind myself that people aren't looking at me or judging me; most people are more concerned with how they look or how they're acting and appearing than they are with how others are appearing. I know that, and yet I still always have the impression that others are staring or laughing at me. The biggest thing I do to ensure my comfort during social events, is to lean on my support: my husband. I'll take his hand or sit with him, and let him be the life of the party with me at his side, feeling less visible and a little more calm.

\*

JANE MCDONALD
Jane was diagnosed with major depressive disorder in 1989,
multiple anxiety disorders in 2001, multiple personality
disorders in 2007, and dissociative identity disorder in 2014

As much as I like to avoid social situations, certain things in life necessitate attending places or events where there are other people. I have a number of strategies to address my anxiety, each with varying levels of success. One strategy is to prepare for potential conversations I might have with people by rehearsing what I would say to someone. For most people, questions like "How are you?" and "What have you been doing?" are normal. But for me they can trigger huge panic, as I never know how to answer without sounding inept. It is difficult to explain in particular to people I don't know why I don't work or go to school, and why I live on social assistance for people with disabilities.

I also can't answer even a basic "Tell me about yourself," without fear of revealing my mental illnesses. I also fear that during a conversation with someone, one of my alters might come out and say something inappropriate.

I also mentally prepare myself before going to places where there will be people by planning. For example, I plan to sit as far back in the bus as I can so that people can't look at me. I plan the order in which to purchase items at a grocery store so that I can get in and out as quickly as possible.

If I enter a situation where I am expected to interact with others, I usually bring a safe person with me. I stick to them like glue and rely on them to recognize signs that I am becoming unwell and to make an excuse to get me out of that situation as soon as possible. I feel it is unfair of me to put this expectation on others, but it is the only way that I can manage to attend social gatherings.

My antianxiety medications also play a large role in my preparation for entering a social domain. Although I try to rely on them as little as possible, I do take them if I know I will be going somewhere where there are a lot of people and where the risk of a panic attack is strong, particularly if I have had such an attack in that place or type of circumstance before. My preference is to try to learn to do these things without the help of medication. I feel it is a skill that I need to learn and which, when learned, will make my life easier. During social engagements, I also try to practice grounding and deep breathing if I can feel myself starting to panic.

*

AMY OWEN
Amy was diagnosed with ADD and
bipolar disorder in 2014 at age 42

I try to tell myself that I can do it. I try to look as good as I can to feel better about myself. I try to go for the people I love, and remind myself this is for them. When I'm there, I stay close to people I know.

I take breaks and go to the bathroom and tell myself I can do this. I put a time limit in place. When I panic, I walk away or ask to leave. I also spend time alone to talk to myself and take a mental break.

*

DENISE PURCELL
Denise was diagnosed with depression, posttraumatic stress disorder, and dissociative identity disorder in 1995 at age 30

I will go and set a time limit. This happens a lot during the holidays. Some people can spend the whole day with each other celebrating. I can't. I have to take it hour by hour, and check in with myself. I have a plan in place with family members about this, and they are pretty good. If they are important in my life, there is always a way to work around it. It's called family and love.

*

ERICKA REEVE
Ericka was diagnosed with dissociative identity disorder, posttraumatic stress disorder, obsessive-compulsive disorder, depression, anxiety and an eating disorder in 2013 at age 26

I always make an attempt to know things far in advance. I need structure—I have to have it. When anything even something small changes, it throws my mind into chaos.

An example of this that comes to mind was a trip to the grocery store two weeks ago. In order to have a successful food shopping trip, I must be able to go through the store the same way I always do, following the pattern of the store in the way I find suitable, visiting the aisles I need to select my items and place them in my basket. Unfortunately, my husband can make this difficult. He typically does not, and he never intends to, but grocery stores are highly triggering

113

for myself and some of my parts. He has wandered off in an attempt to help so we could leave sooner, as he knows it can be a struggle. In doing this, however, we became frantic because I couldn't find him. I turned around and suddenly he was gone. Some of my parts thought he left us, never to return. He does not fully know the extent of this particular issue, but he saw how distressed I was and we left as soon as possible. One of my parts came in a bit more, creating a soothing comfort of co-consciousness, meaning one or more of us is present and "fronting," a.k.a. in control of my body at the same time. You can imagine that this gets tricky, but we make it work.

*

LORRAINE SCOTT
Lorraine was diagnosed with non-epilepsy attack disorder
and dissociative identity disorder in 2016 at age 48

If I've got to attend a social engagement, we have to preplan and make sure we have everything in place. It depends on the engagement as to how much we have to plan, but some of the things we do is as follows:

- Book a hotel, depending on the length of the journey and timeframe of the engagement.

- A wheelchair is needed if a lot of walking is involved. I push myself to walk to get exercise, but once the pain starts, it means I have to get out the wheelchair. This is a sign I've put too much stress on my spine and that is causing only more damage, and could result in a week in bed and even more severe pain.

- My pillow, so that if I conk out or have a seizure in the car, I can be made comfortable, as this always causes neck pain. A pillow helps provide support.

- Pain medication, as walking amplifies the pain to a point where sitting, lying, or standing is all painful.

- I also carry my medical file. It has hospital letters, notes about my seizures, conking out and blackouts, previous and future appointments, and a list of medications. This is just in case I need medical attention when out of town.

- I carry an iPad to help prevent seizures or conking out during the car journey. It keeps my eyes focused, and away from the window, because passing trees and other vehicles appear as flashing because of the speed in which they're moving.

- My iPhone has all my important contacts, and is used as a backup for games to keep me sidetracked.

When in a social setting, I'm okay with interacting for thirty minutes, up to a couple of hours. However, this is not always the case as stated before. It depends on the setting, noise levels, lighting if any, my stress levels, if I'm alert or if I'm tired, and if I'm in pain. All these play a role as to if and how long I can be in a social or public setting of any kind. After a few minutes of conversations, my mind will go blank and I will have long stares, my eyes will look drained and then my head will jolt. I will have long pauses between words, slur my speech, experience pain in my head, aching or itchy eyes, and become overly excited. These are all the warning signs that a seizure, blackout or conk out is going to happen, and we know that we need to get me home or to a safe place. Once these start, we will say that I'm feeling unwell and about to have a seizure so need to get home or back to the hotel. Most people are very understanding, but some don't really understand. Some will offer assistance, while others just stare at you.

When telling some friends and family, it wasn't until they experienced me having an episode and saw how I came out of it and how traumatizing it was for me. This has now stopped those from pushing me to attend nights out or parties. Now, I can choose if I attend parties or functions, and that will depend on how my day goes and how many seizures I've had during the day, and the state I am in when I come out of them. It's nice not having that emotional pressure put on you, because people look at you and think you're okay. I always say to people that just because I look good on the outside, it doesn't mean that I'm good on the inside, so don't judge what you see, learn the facts before making a judgment.

This can be very stressful for me when people are constantly expecting you to be able to join in with functions and group parties and group holidays or any holiday. It's very difficult for me to plan anything with this illness, but I'm not letting the illness take over. I know what I can cope with and my triggers, and it doesn't matter how much you tell some people, it's like they don't listen to what you're saying. On the flip side, there's those who want to help me enjoy life, and that's why they want to include me in the things they do. I'm fine with that, and I do try my best to join in with social activities, functions, and group parties, but I won't be forced if I'm not up to it. I know when to draw the line, rest, and keep myself safe from dangers of triggers and other stress that can bring on any of my symptoms. I'm not going to risk making myself more ill for the sake of socializing.

These illnesses can at times be very embarrassing for me, especially the seizures, conking out, and blackouts. I don't think people realize how embarrassing it is for me and the emotional impact it has on me. When I'm out shopping, I have to use the wheelchair most of the time, and people just stare at you as they go by. This is upsetting every time someone looks at me, not knowing why and what they are thinking makes it even worse. It's very difficult to handle that, but I do try to ignore it and just have fun and enjoy being out and about.

*

CARRIE WORTHINGTON
Carrie was diagnosed with depression,
anxiety, and trichotillomania in 2000 at age 41

Most social engagements do not affect me because of my illness any longer. The only thing, like I mentioned before, is making sure I am not the only one without a partner. I have become very aware of not being a couple, and I have avoided some gatherings if I am unsure of the makeup of the group. It makes me anxious enough that I just avoid the activities. When I have been somewhere where everyone was coupled but me, it has resulted in throwing me into sadness, and the loss and grief come back. This state of mind may just be the aftermath, or it may last for a few days and causes me to isolate. I have been trying to go places on my own, which causes a huge amount of anxiety, but I have been able to not react to those feelings that I can't do it, and I have been able to face some things I have avoided. In fact, I recently went to a small concert venue at the local university to see an artist by myself. The whole time before it was time to go, I was anxious, and my inner self was not sure I could do it. I did go out and I am so grateful I turned the negative thoughts around and went. I was not uncomfortable at the venue, during intermission, sitting alone. As I was walking to the car, I was just feeling joy, because I thoroughly enjoyed myself, and that was a great accomplishment for me.

*

Start where you are. Use what you have.
Do what you can.
ARTHUR ASHE

\*

CHAPTER EIGHT

# Coping with Triggers

Ideas come from somewhere. People don't come
up with these ideas from nowhere. Something
triggers your thoughts. -LAZARO HERNANDEZ

Triggers, events that threaten our stability, are something that those
of us living with mental illness manage on a daily basis. Some triggers
can cause a panic attack or PTSD flashback. For others, a prolonged
intense situation can trigger a depressive episode. Identifying and
coping with known triggers is an important part of ensuring our well-
being. What are your triggers and how do you manage them?

*

ADRIANNE ALLEN-LANG
Adrianne was diagnosed with dissociative
identity disorder in 2015 at age 18

Yelling, violence, things been thrown, large crowds, strangers,
the smell of breast milk, being cornered or restrained, blood, etc. We
deal with them through mindfulness and breathing techniques. It's
okay these days as through therapy, it has been getting easier to cope

with, resulting in being triggered less frequently, but severe anxiety is still there around the events and during them.

*

MORGAN BUTLER
Morgan was diagnosed with depression
and anxiety in 2009 at age 15

Depression triggers include when others express disappointment in me, or say certain things that express that they don't believe in me. Physical triggers sometimes occur when I see others self-mutilate. Sometimes I'm not aware of a trigger, and just feel awful. When it happens, I can't stop the looming feeling from sweeping over me.

When it comes to anxiety, it's a constant. There are just some moments when I suddenly think that I won't be safe driving home, that something bad will happen. Sometimes somebody will say something to me that I misinterpreted, and I will think about what I could have said or done differently, worrying about it for days on end.

When it comes to physical triggers, my depression is at its worst in the winter, which I mainly attribute to the weather and lack of rest. When I am rejected over something, it triggers my depression and anxiety, and I question my purpose and self-worth. My anxiety is also triggered by certain settings. Some days I'm perfectly fine in crowds, others, I can barely be around friends.

The best way to minimize any of these is by stepping away from the situation, if physically near the trigger. Sometimes going for a walk, listening to music, praying, or just being around my dog can help. I definitely recommend getting an animal, if that's up your alley. I didn't even realize how much I depended on my dog for support, until recently when I had a breakdown in my kitchen and my dog jumped into my lap. It's incredible how much better you feel after crying on your furry friend's shoulder, especially if human interaction was your recent trigger.

\*

LYNDA CHELDELIN FELL
Lynda was diagnosed with depression in 2000 at age 35
and posttraumatic stress disorder in 2012 at age 47

My main depressive trigger is seasonal change. I'm a sweater girl at heart, so September and October are my favorite months. But the changing of the seasons means less daylight hours, more rain and—most triggering of all—the heralding in of the holiday season.

I grew up with traditional holiday festivities. I loved everything about it: the home décor, twinkling Christmas lights, fragrant candles, and warm, freshly baked holiday treats. It was truly a magical time in my childhood, and something I carried on for my own kids. So much so that Aly, our daughter, and I had our Christmas tree up and fully decorated in September. We adored the holiday season, and Christmas music began playing throughout the house as soon as our tree was up. While some think that's nuts, I never understood those who put in all that time and effort for four short weeks in December.

When Aly was killed, the holidays lost their magic and became a stark reminder of life at its darkest. My world was filled suddenly with unimaginable pain. I went through the motions of the holidays simply because the family counted on it, but personally I just wanted to skip life entirely until January. The holiday season has since resumed their cheerfulness, yet will always remain tinged with bittersweet pain. I love the magic of the season and do experience many moments of joy, but come September and October my heart is heavy with nostalgia from past holidays when my family was whole.

From a PTSD standpoint, I live with a constant trigger that has yet to ease. Our remaining children are now adults, but anytime I know they're in their car, I am absolutely terrified. It's been over seven years since losing Aly in a car accident, and one would think this would have calmed down by now. But it hasn't. I can't bubble wrap my children, nor do I prevent them from experiencing a blessed life. But I hold my breath anytime I know they're traveling in a car.

About two years after losing Aly, our oldest daughter and our four-year-old grandson rolled their vehicle on the freeway one snowy day. She wasn't too sure about the weather, and called home to ask her dad whether she should turn around. While in mid-sentence on the phone, her car hit a patch of ice on the freeway and rolled multiple times into the median. My husband heard the entire accident over the phone, and frantically began yelling her name. She could hear her dad yelling, but couldn't see anything or find her phone because of the deployed airbag. My husband stayed on the phone with her until medics arrived on scene. Distressed and shaken, we quickly jumped into our car to begin the forty-five minute drive through fresh snowfall toward the hospital. Thankfully, the snow had cushioned the car's rolls, and neither our daughter or grandson were hurt, though our daughter's car was a total loss.

To this day, I experience near panic when I know my children are driving somewhere. It's been seven years since our youngest daughter died in a car accident, and five years since our oldest rolled her car, but the panic hasn't yet eased. I understand that this is part of the PTSD, but I'm still hoping it won't be with me for life.

*

SHAUNA COX
Shauna was diagnosed with an
anxiety disorder in 2009 at age 26

There are three big triggers that are sure to cause anxiety for me: crowds, line-ups, and not being with my husband, Roger. I'll explain each of them in turn.

Crowds are a trigger for me whether it be a crowd at a party (even if I know a lot of the people there and especially if I don't), at a mall, or a big event like a concert or a hockey game. If I know that I am attending something or going somewhere where there will be a lot of people, I feel anxious just at the thought of going and the anxiety increases the closer I get to being in the crowd. Unfortunately, a lot of the time I engage in avoidance, especially when it comes to social gatherings where I don't know a lot of the people in attendance.

As an example, my husband often competes in ball tournaments. We bring our camper and camp with whatever team he happens to be playing with. A lot of the time, this involves camping with a lot of people who I've either never met or who I don't know well. When it comes time to socializing after the games, I often find myself literally paralyzed in anxious fear. I don't know whether to sit or stand, who to sit or stand with , or how to start up a conversation. If I do start talking to someone, I'm overanalyzing everything that I say during and after the conversation. I worry that I'll say or do something that makes me look stupid. And so, a lot of the time, I hide out in the camper until my husband comes in after me and encourages me outside with him. I want to be outside with the group, but it's as if my body finds it hard to cooperate; it's seemingly impossible to shake off the anxiety enough to venture out on my own.

When I do end up going somewhere where there a lot of people, there are several strategies that I will undertake to cope and, even, have fun. One strategy is to fall back on medication. I will take an anxiolytic beforehand to calm my nerves. Another strategy is to take along someone I'm comfortable with like my husband or a close friend. I will also visualize the event going well beforehand, and push out any negative thoughts. If I do think of negative scenarios, I make sure to think of strategies to overcome them. A lot of the time, I end up realizing that the worst-case scenario really isn't so bad, which makes it that much easier to face. At the event, I will use calming breaths if I start to feel anxious, I will clear my mind at times, and I will use my trusty mantra: "How it was in the past is not how it is now," reminding me of how far I've come and that I will be okay. Afterwards, if I catch myself overanalyzing something I said that I perceive as embarrassing, I'll remind myself that other people probably didn't notice it as embarrassing and even if they did, they probably forgot it ten seconds after it occurred.

The second trigger is line-ups. Grocery stores, malls, and airports are places that are sure to have line-ups and almost guaranteed to have me feeling at least a bit of anxiety, even now that I'm a million times better than I once was. The issue that I have with line-ups are the illusion that I can't make an easy escape from them if I needed or wanted to. If there's someone behind me in line at the grocery store, I can't just leave a basket of things in front of them, and it's even worse if my items are on the conveyor belt. If I'm at the airport, getting out of line for a last minute bathroom trip because my body is screaming flight (pun not intended!), risks me missing the plane. When it comes to airports, I still fall back on taking an anxiolytic. I also use some of the same strategies I use to overcome being in crowds. For grocery shopping or trips to the mall, I think back to past visits and that when I have left the situation, I suddenly feel better. Knowing that allows me to realize that it really is in my head, that the anxiety will pass, and that helps calm me down.

Finally, being without my husband is a trigger. This might sound like a weird trigger, so allow me to explain. My biggest fear is being without my husband in life. Every time he goes out, I worry that it is the last time I will see him. When he goes to work, if he goes to a friend's house, if he drives to another town for a baseball tournament, I worry that he will get into an accident and die. I worry so badly that sometimes I will make myself cry, thinking the worst. One of my psychologists helped me realize that I can't control everything and she encouraged me to put positive thoughts into the universe. I don't know how much of that I believe in, but it does help to calm me down from hyperventilating cry sessions after Roger leaves the house. I'll imagine my love and protection floating out to him, and I'll distract myself through working, reading, watching television, or any number of things to occupy my mind on something else. There are still times, however, when I ask him to text or call when he arrives somewhere so that I know he got there safe. He knows how much I worry, and so he will remind me not to panic if I don't hear from him when anticipated. In these instances, I try not to look at the time so that I don't even know when he's later than expected.

I don't know if these will always be triggers for me, but I'd like to think that someday I can be in a crowd, stand in a line, or be without Roger and not feel any anxiety. Distracting myself seems to be the best strategy I've found so far, and the more good experiences I have in these situations, the greater the chance that I will win over the anxiety.

\*

JANE MCDONALD
Jane was diagnosed with major depressive disorder in 1989,
multiple anxiety disorders in 2001, multiple personality
disorders in 2007, and dissociative identity disorder in 2014

Crowds are a major trigger for me because of my avoidant personality disorder and social anxiety disorder. It can be a crowd at a grocery store, a movie theater, or a group of people at a library. Even having a full waiting room at my doctor's office can be triggering for me. I am always afraid that people are looking at me and judging me. I fear that I look the wrong way, do or say the wrong thing and look stupid, inept, immature, or otherwise inadequate. I constantly fear the judgment and subsequent ridicule of others.

I know that I have never been comfortable in a group of people and have always been introverted, but this fear largely emerged after being bullied extensively throughout elementary school. I constantly worry that people will laugh at me, tease me, ridicule me, make fun of me, or judge me. As a result, I tend to avoid any kind of social situation, or at least I do as much as possible.

When I have to enter a crowd, say a waiting room or public transit, I try to practice deep breathing and find something to distract me and draw attention away from the crowd of people such as a game on my cell phone, or a book I can read. If the crowd is particularly large, I will take antianxiety medication beforehand to help curb my anxiety and make me less fearful.

I also find loud, sudden, or unexpected sounds to be very triggering. As a result of my anxiety and PTSD I suffer from hyper-arousal and am constantly vigilant for new noises or sounds, and subsequently have an exaggerated startle response. I do my best to avoid places where there might be loud noises, but this isn't always possible, particularly as I live next to both a fire station and ambulance station. When loud noises occur I practice taking deep breaths and positive self-talk, telling myself that I am okay and it is just a noise, and that I am not in immediate danger. If one of my other personalities is out, however, she is very difficult to calm down and often will try to find a quiet corner and rock herself.

Another trigger for me seems to be certain people who resemble one of my abusers. A stranger on the street who reminds me of my abuser can lead to flashbacks and abject fear that I'll be harmed once again. Rationally, I know this is a different individual and that I am safe, but the fear is visceral and difficult to avoid. This is difficult to deal with, as you cannot control who you will run into at any given time. The only way to prevent this is to remain hidden away in my apartment which, I am sad to say, is something I have often had to resort to. Even then, though, I am not completely safe. Often, a picture will come up online, either on the internet in general or on Facebook, of a male who fits that description. The mayor of my own city matches this description, and while I want to be kept appraised of the goings on in the city, it is very difficult to be confronted with pictures of him all the time.

Another difficult person to avoid who fits this description is my own psychiatrist. I have worked very hard to reassure my youngest alter that he is a "safe" person and will not harm her. From what my psychiatrist tells me, she is becoming gradually less afraid of him and tries to engage more rather than cower in fear like she first did. Still, seeing him, or others who look like him, can be enough to trigger a huge fear reaction, leading to uncontrollable shaking, curling into a ball in a corner, and trying to hide (from what I am told and from the positions I find myself in). I try very hard to create positive, or at least neutral, experiences with people whose appearances are distressing and triggering, and have had limited success. Again, it is a trigger that is often difficult to avoid.

Sometimes music can be a very strong trigger, both for me and several of my other personalities. The trouble with this particular trigger is that while certain types of music are triggering for some alters, particularly Christian pop music, the same music is able to calm down my littlest alter, and tends to work better than most other strategies for calming her. She is triggered by what I call angry music, like heavy metal or rock, which is what my angrier alter tends to like and put on. I haven't really figured out a way to handle these triggers, except to try to play only Christian music when I feel my youngest one coming out, and to never play rock or heavy metal myself, which is difficult because it is music that I enjoy and grew up listening to.

Other times it is not necessarily the genre of music, but the content and lyrics of particular songs. Lady Gaga, for instance, recently performed a song called "Til It Happens to You," about sexual violence on college and university campuses. Although my own experiences were in high school, this song can still be very triggering for me and lead to flashbacks. I try to avoid listening to it, but it does come on the radio occasionally and I have to turn it off. However, these efforts are often too little too late, and I find myself in the midst of emotional turmoil.

Interestingly, at other times, when I am feeling "stronger" (for lack of a better term), I like to listen to these songs because it reminds me that I am a survivor rather than a victim.

When I am myself, I feel more or less able to cope with triggers. I know how to ground myself most of the time, how to distract from things, and other distress management techniques that I have learned over the years in various therapy programs.

My primary concern is what triggers my youngest alter, because I am not always aware of what is happening, and therefore can't help her. Also, because she does not speak, it is difficult for others to understand what is happening or what is upsetting her. If I feel her coming out and getting upset, I try to do what I can for her in terms of soothing music, teddy bears, coloring, blankets, etc., but sometimes it's not enough. At the moment, I'm researching communication tools used by nonverbal individuals to convey to others what they are thinking, feeling, and experiencing. I haven't found anything yet, but it is something I am working on. I am learning how to ground myself, to try to stay in the present, but it is very much something I am still working on and learning.

*

AMY OWEN
Amy was diagnosed with ADD and
bipolar disorder in 2014 at age 42

My trigger is feeling pressured to do something I'm not comfortable with. Just waking up and thinking about getting through the day, or being put in a spot when I'm not prepared or don't feel ready. I try to breathe. I try to tell myself it's not the end of the world if I don't get it right. I also tell myself nobody is perfect, including me. So I can do better next time.

*

DENISE PURCELL
Denise was diagnosed with depression, posttraumatic stress
disorder, and dissociative identity disorder in 1995 at age 30

I have different triggers at different times. In an ordinary day, something like smelling aftershave that my abuser wore can make me sick and cause extreme panic. Coffee breath. I know that sounds funny but it is a distinct smell, like the aftershave, that affects me. Large man hands are another trigger. I have to look at the hands of a man when I talk to him, no matter who it is. If he has big hands, I feel threatened and scared. I try to focus on what's around me and to be in the present moment, but that's really hard because my mind will go right back to the abuse and get stuck.

*

ERICKA REEVE
Ericka was diagnosed with dissociative identity disorder,
posttraumatic stress disorder, obsessive-compulsive disorder,
depression, anxiety and an eating disorder in 2013 at age 26

Everything. No kidding. It's exhausting. It seems to be that on any given day, something can be triggering that wasn't only a few days ago, but now creates a "hell on Earth" scenario. I have one part who can help me with grounding myself. She, by way of explanation, controls and assists my movements. She'll begin to rub my jeans or mess with a fidget toy to help me begin to stabilize. I can now begin doing this on my own if I notice in time. The grocery store, sleep, doctors, smells, tastes, sights, and even some medications and their individual scents can be highly triggering for some of my parts and myself. One of my troubles is that I do not yet know all of my triggers, and so when something arises, it can be difficult to pinpoint the problem.

*

LORRAINE SCOTT
Lorraine was diagnosed with non-epilepsy attack disorder
and dissociative identity disorder in 2016 at age 48

All of my illnesses have varying triggers, depending on the setting, environment, and people. These are just a few, but my body and mindset can be triggers too, like when I haven't had enough sleep, in a lot of pain, stressing, or even overly excited. These can trigger seizures, conking out, and blackouts along with noise, motion, and flashing lights, or anything else flashing. Being in pain, whether physically or emotionally, feeling threatened, at risk, upset, unwanted, or unloved will trigger protection Lorraine. This is my brain's way of coping with the stresses and trauma. We all have a protective mechanism, it's just mine is slightly different due to the amount of trauma I have experienced. Many other people out there including some who are reading this will be able to relate.

Setting: At home, if I go into a room and things are out of place, or maybe someone left a cup on the coffee table from the night before, my anger will go from zero to a hundred within minutes, and trigger a switch. If the person isn't around, I will stew about it until they are. By this time my stress level is high and angry Lorraine will give them a verbal bashing. My heart rate and blood pressure rise, and before you know it, I'm having pain in my head followed by a seizure, or conk out and then a seizure. Little things like this can be huge, and be the onset of instability. So my prevention is to tell those around me what my triggers are to help avoid and minimize the risks at home. This doesn't always pan out because people forget and some don't know, so I'm constantly having to say and remind those at home to keep everything in its place.

Motion and Environment: When going out, chances are that during the car journey, I may have conked out, had an absent seizure or another type of seizure. This will occur because of the speed the car is moving, and the trees, vehicles, houses all flashing by. To help minimize this, I have window shades. These will black out the side windows so I don't see much of the flashing, but I will still conk out because of the motion. This was happening every time I got into a car, but I am learning ways to help lessen the amount of times this happens. By the time I get to where I'm going, we are never sure of what state of mind I will be in, so I always (for safety reasons) have one of my kids with me, as they are my safe network. When I'm outdoors, shopping, or having a meal in a pub, those environments can trigger seizures because of the noise level when busy. So, as I've stated before, these are just some of the environments in which the two-hour limit will be put in motion; although normally after an hour there are signs that I'm going downhill, sometimes more rapidly than others. My preventions are to not stay. As soon as I get the feeling of being drained, I will alert those I'm with so we can quickly finish up what we're doing and get me home.

People: I get along great with people and I used to be okay in group settings, although sometimes I prefer one-on-one, as then I can just focus on one person. When groups of people are talking or there are a lot of conversations going on, my mind struggles to focus on just one, otherwise it sounds like a lot of scrambled conversations. This causes confusion and will also trigger the pain in my head. When I go to speak during a conversation that's been going on for a half hour or more, I may start to struggle getting words out, and it feels like my mouth is having a spasm, although this isn't noticed because it happens so quickly. I will also slur my words and start to find it difficult to remember which words I wanted to say and what the conversation is all about. These are all signs that I am about to conk out, so yes, it's time to get me to the car and home. I find that this totally exhausts me and I could be conked out for the rest of the day or longer.

I do try to prevent group settings, but I'm comfortable around those who know about my illnesses and have experienced them, so I know I'm in good hands. However, I do not let this stop me from being in other group settings or around other people. It does drain me when I am around new people because I am trying so hard to hold back from conking out, blacking out, or having a seizure; and I am trying hard to focus on the conversations and so this, believe it or not, is very exhausting for me mentally and will again trigger my episodes. It's very difficult but I do try to be in a social environment each week just not to let this beat me. I am a fighter of illnesses. Whether I'm going to win or not, I will not back down.

Noise: It can be any noise from music to crying babies. It's all noise and all sounds load in my head and will cause me to conk out, followed by a seizure.

Flashing lights and brightness: I try to avoid lights which cause a blindness feeling. As for flashing lights or flashing of trees and vehicles, these will all cause me to conk out and have an episode of seizures. My preventions are sunscreens on the car doors, focusing on something relaxing like playing games to keep my mind active and distracted from the lights or flashing. Even talking in the car can cause me to conk out. I've done this so many times in the middle of a conversation, it's unbelievable. I'm just grateful that I have a great support network of people around me that just say "She's gone off" when this happens, and they always check regularly that I'm breathing and comfortable. If I do attend a party or other setting that has flashing lights, I will check first if there is a room on the premises where there are no flashing lights. If there isn't another room, I will stay toward the back of the room away from the lights, make sure someone sits in front of me to block out the flashing lights, and I will leave the room after fifteen-minute intervals. This doesn't always work and therefore I could be on the floor within the first half hour, but those are the preventions that I have in place for those circumstances.

Moods/Excitement: I try to make sure I don't get too excited, as "Bang, there she goes on the floor, knocked out." The ones closest to me know what's coming, and will make sure I'm safe from hurting myself. I do avoid alcohol and rarely drink, but if I do, I have a watered down lemonade spritzer of three parts lemonade to one part rose wine, sometimes half part rose and three and a half parts lemonade. I just want to keep away any dangers that I can and avoid putting myself at more risk of dangerous things happening to me.

I can also get so excited that the next day I'm on a downer, but I think that is me switching personalities because I've become overly excited and the switch is to protect me from getting hurt. It's like even though I'm excited and happy about something, my brain knows that something or someone is going to do something to hurt me, and to protect me it will switch to protection and guard mode.

It's pretty awesome how the brain works, and having dissociative identity disorder shows that the brain has extra potential. I also avoid being around people who may want to cause trouble or may be horrible to others. I will walk away if I'm in a situation where someone wants to cause trouble. I've spent over thirty years avoiding anger and trouble. I don't like it, and I know if someone were to start on me, I would switch to aggressive Lorraine and I do not like her. I've managed for years to keep her locked away and I want her to stay there, behind lock and key. I really don't like aggression or aggressive people and it scares me to be around anyone who's getting aggressive.

Sleep deprivation: Lack of sleep is a no-no for me, although there are times when I can't sleep due to my pain killers. If this happens, I'll conk out anyway so one way or another I'll be out of it. This is another trigger for me and my seizures.

*

CARRIE WORTHINGTON
Carrie was diagnosed with depression,
anxiety, and trichotillomania in 2000 at age 41

When I'm struggling from depression associated with grief, being in certain situations will be a trigger. Being with couples where it is obvious I am the single makes me sad, and still dealing with my grief, alone and unhappy. Not too many other things recently have been triggers. If I am exercising as I should, keeping busy by being productive at home, volunteering, or going to school, this has helped avoid any triggers or situations that may cause anxiety. Worrying about the future of my job has triggered anxiety, however with five years of therapy, I now have the tools to deal with this. I have not had a full-blown panic attack in two years, and have been able to keep the high anxiety to a very brief moment. I have started a gratitude journal to write three or four short sentences about my day. They are usually positive, although sometimes fear and not really happy things find their way into the book. It's a way to look at what happened that day, and start fresh the next morning. Always looking at the positive, appreciating nature, the beauty of a sunrise or my grandchildren's faces has helped keep the depression at a very minimum these days.

Sad hurts but it's a healthy feeling. It is a necessary
thing to feel. Depression is very different.
*

# CHAPTER NINE

# Managing Daily Life

Being in control of your life and having realistic expectations about your day-to-day challenges are the keys to stress management, which is perhaps the most important ingredient to living a happy, healthy and rewarding life. -MARILU HENNER

Scientists studying mental illness have zeroed in on the body's stress response. When the body reacts to stressors, the endocrine system produces stress hormones which then impact our immune function. Unlike most people, activities of daily living can cause extra stress for those living with a mental illness. What strategies do you use to manage daily life?

*

ADRIANNE ALLEN-LANG
Adrianne was diagnosed with dissociative
identity disorder in 2015 at age 18

I find in my daily life, the hardest thing is remembering to care for myself. I spend all my time making sure my son is okay. I often go days without eating or showering because I forget to, or I function with only four hours of sleep because my alters keep me awake or I keep having nightmares. I try to make sure to set reminders on my phone to eat, take medications, shower, go to bed, etc., otherwise I just neglect all of my necessities because I'm unable to register that it is what I need at that time.

*

MORGAN BUTLER
Morgan was diagnosed with depression
and anxiety in 2009 at age 15

For the most part, keeping busy is the best way to keep my mind at bay. This means either booking my day completely, or just going home from work and crafting or making art, baking, or even binge-watching TV shows on Netflix to decompress. Sometimes I'll find time to take my dog on a long walk or hike, or go for a drive. Even a brief bit of fresh air can change my perspective on my day or situation. I just have to keep busy and step back from any stressors.

*

LYNDA CHELDELIN FELL
Lynda was diagnosed with depression in 2000 at age 35
and posttraumatic stress disorder in 2012 at age 47

I manage by taking excellent care of myself. I walk every morning, eat healthy and holistically, and practice good sleep hygiene. My work is fulfilling and rewarding. I stick to a routine as much as possible and surround myself with love and laughter. When I notice even a hint of depressive symptoms, I schedule an appointment with my doctor. I know my body. I know my symptoms. I'm proactive in taking care of myself.

\*

SHAUNA COX
Shauna was diagnosed with an
anxiety disorder in 2009 at age 26

I used to feel a high amount of anxiety at work, but that has improved with time. At my old job as an administrative assistant at a funeral home, I actually had my psychologist write a letter to my boss explaining my anxiety disorder because I felt it could hinder my performance at times. I am a hard worker, and very conscientious, and looking back on it I know that I didn't have anything to worry about in terms of my job. When I was in the thick of the anxiety disorder, however, I couldn't see that. All I could see were the moments when I felt hot, sweaty, nauseous, and had to race to the bathroom, and I felt like I was failing at my job because of that. I was so worried that I would have to go to the bathroom when alone in the building and that I would get in trouble for leaving the reception area. I was worried that I would have an accident if I didn't go, and how embarrassing would that be? My psychologist asked me how many times I was actually left alone in the building. Not very often. How many times had I had an accident? Never. These fears I had were so irrational, but for some reason it was hard for me to realize that.

Fast forward to the present, and I'm now a receptionist for a vet clinic. There are still moments when old feelings and fears wash over me when I'm alone in the front, but I'm better at talking myself through it. "It's okay," I'll say to myself. "How it was in the past is not how it is now." It's a mantra my psychologist taught me to help calm myself down. I'll tell myself that it won't be long before someone can come help me. If things get really bad and I have to run to the bathroom, I quickly tell someone and go. It's not the end of the world.

Part of my issue with anxiety is that everything to me seems like it will be the end of the world. If I make a mistake at work, I stress about it nonstop. I have trouble letting things go and forgiving myself. Deep down I know that I won't get fired for minor mistakes, but it's hard not to beat myself up and feel anxious at the stupidity of the mistake. And yet, if I'm supervising someone and they accidentally do something wrong, it's not a big deal. It's hard to see that it's the same with myself. In a way, I guess my anxiety about making mistakes has made me a bit of a perfectionist.

I know that I have to learn to let things go so that I am not so stressed and anxious all the time. When I come home from work, I try to clear my mind and relax. I do something that I enjoy like reading or writing, watching television, going for a walk, or spending time with my husband and our pets. When I am at work, I try to remember not to take everything so seriously. I socialize with my coworkers and have fun, and keep my mantra at the ready for when I feel panic-like attacks start to bubble up.

Another daily living stressor for me involves money. I love doing our budget every month, but my husband hates it because he is confronted with my anxiety. I am so afraid of not having any money to pay bills that I overanalyze every little thing that we spend money on. If there's a three dollar charge on our debit card and neither of us can remember what it's for, I start to panic. I know that three dollars is minimal in the grand scheme of our budget, and that we always figure out what this mystery charge might be, but in the moment all I can think of is that if we continue to buy things that we can't remember, we will go bankrupt! I know this is irrational, but my heart races at the thought, and even when we're not actively working on our budget, there are times when I find myself stressing nonstop about how much money we have in the bank, upcoming bills, and whether or not we can afford to live! While my husband and I aren't rich by any means, we are doing okay and so this is not a realistic concern that I should be thinking about as often as I am. There are more times than I'd care to admit where I've actually felt myself losing the ability to take deep breaths because of how panicked I am at the thought of spending money. When I feel myself getting worked up in this instance, I try as hard as I can to take a deep breath and to let those thoughts slip away. My husband helps with this as well in pointing out that we are doing well, we are both at good, stable jobs, and we are spending our money wisely. He also helps me to see that in the long run, having each other is more important than anything else. Once again, I am reminded by how much it helps to have loved ones in your life when you are dealing with a mental illness.

*

JANE MCDONALD
Jane was diagnosed with major depressive disorder in 1989, multiple anxiety disorders in 2001, multiple personality disorders in 2007, and dissociative identity disorder in 2014

Tasks of daily living have always been difficult for me. Things like even getting out of bed, showering, getting dressed, and even eating can be unmanageable at times. Some days are better. I wake up earlier, shower, get dressed, brush my teeth and hair, do my makeup, and even leave my apartment to go to appointments or do leisure activities. Unfortunately, these days are few and far between. Many days I'll get up before nine or so, but struggle to do even basic self-care activities, let alone any kind of cleaning, organizing, or even leave my apartment. My depression and anxiety are large contributing factors.

To try to cope with these tasks, I have tried to set goals for each day, writing them out on paper and sticking them to my fridge. I try to reward myself occasionally if I am able to do things like get out of my apartment or even manage to get showered and dressed each day of the week. Also, leaving the apartment even for a five-minute walk is difficult due to physical challenges and limitations. Occasionally, I will tell myself that I can only watch a certain movie or tv show if I accomplish the goals for that day or week. At other times, I set up long-term rewards with my case manager, such as going for a walk at a local conservation area with her. Other things I can use to reward myself are listening to my favorite music, doing art, or having a conversation or visit with a friend. It is difficult for me, however, to maintain the willpower necessary to only do these things when I have met my goals and, thus, I often end up caving and watching my shows, listening to my music, or having a special treat to eat even when I have not met these goals.

*

AMY OWEN
Amy was diagnosed with ADD and
bipolar disorder in 2014 at age 42

I stress out about the day. I worry to the extreme about my kids and if I am being a good enough mom. So I start my day early to get through my bad thoughts. I look at my kids and see the love they have for me and push myself to do what is right for them. I do fun things with them so we all can relax. I do a lot of self-talk and push myself as hard as I can to make the ones I love happy. That makes me happy.

*

DENISE PURCELL

Denise was diagnosed with depression, posttraumatic stress
disorder, and dissociative identity disorder in 1995 at age 30

Getting up, getting to sleep, doing pretty much anything right
now is hard. It comes in spurts. I'm on a low cycle now and don't care
about much. Not to say that I don't care about people, because I do. I
don't know how to care for myself, or love myself. I can for anyone
else but me. I have a hard time feeling like life is real when I'm in this
state. I do what I have to in order to get by and not deal with people
complaining. So I guess you could say I hide how I feel as to not upset
others.

*

ERICKA REEVE

Ericka was diagnosed with dissociative identity disorder,
posttraumatic stress disorder, obsessive-compulsive disorder,
depression, anxiety and an eating disorder in 2013 at age 26

I think speaking to relatives would be the easiest answer to this.
Daily living is pretty basic most days for me and my parts. My guess is
it looks very similar to anyone else's. We wake up, I orient myself, get
ready, we then care for our ferrets, giving everyone food and water.
We make sure they're clean and well cared for. One of my younger
parts is typically on top of this.

Myself or Minny (a nurturing mother-type part) will try to stay
on top of the laundry and dishes, making sure our needs are met and
that we are all doing well. I'll work on writing a few pieces and putting
together various things we need, and chitchat in the afternoons with
my husband before he leaves for work. Strategies I (or we) use tend to
be all of the above things, actually. If Minny is concerned for us, I

know the house will then be immaculate. If we are particularly stressed out or anxious, I now know that the weasels will be out and as playful as ever. Something new will be created and that has helped to calm them, in turn soothing me. We work together on all things now.

\*

LORRAINE SCOTT
Lorraine was diagnosed with non-epilepsy attack disorder
and dissociative identity disorder in 2016 at age 48

My daily life has changed tremendously. There are a lot of things that I can no longer do, and it's been very difficult for me to come to terms with all this, as I was a very independent, hardworking single mother. I was thriving in my career before I became ill, and in the end, I could no longer work as I was a risk to the company by having uncontrolled, unpredictable and regular seizures. I could no longer drive, either and I felt like I lost everything I had worked so hard for. I value my children, they are my life. They are why I worked so hard and in saying that, I knew that I had to embrace this as it wasn't just upsetting me, it was also upsetting them. They were frightened, as none of us knew what was going on. As my illness got worse, my children never wanted to leave me and even seven years later they still don't. This caused us all extra stress and it is still going on now, seven years later. I've gone through a lot of different emotions until I partly came to terms with this as my new life. We all have to make changes at some point in life, and this was my time. I had to embrace this, as I really had no control over what was happening to me. The last thing I wanted to do was put anyone else at risk or upset and worry my family and close friends. This was and still is all-around a very frightening time for me and my children. I could no longer drive, work, workout, go for walks, stand for more than a couple of minutes, cook, make drinks, bake, sew, attend courses, do household chores, or my gardening. All of these things I loved doing so much. I had just had a new car and after a couple of times driving, I was told I wasn't allowed to drive anymore. I was devastated. My illness was getting worse as the days and weeks went on, and I started to suffer from memory loss to the point where I didn't know my kids, who I was, or our home, either. This was and still is such a bad time for us all, and I hate being told that I didn't know my kids. It's heartbreaking every time this happens.

Some people think that those who don't work enjoy staying at home doing nothing, but this isn't the case. I hate it with a passion and I would be out there still working if I could. I've always been a worker, constantly on the go working, learning, and achieving, along with being dedicated to my kids. I always tried to better myself throughout my life and even since being ill, I've taken a couple of online courses which I can pick up when and as I'm up to it. As the years have gone by, people talk less to you and eventually they just fade away, but for every friendship that has faded away a new one is made. It's horrible sitting at home going one day to the next not talking to anyone but your children and their friends. I have friends who have said that if I ever need or want to talk to just contact them. But when I do, they may not have time for my problems, or maybe they don't want my problems getting them down. These are the ones who fade away in the end. When this started to happen, I knew I had to find something to keep my mind active, as I didn't want to drop into depression as I had been warned by my brother-in-law. So, I decided I would try and do some sewing and crafts, this way I could stop and start when and as I could, and when I felt an episode coming on, I could just go lie down and sleep it off. There are times I've been found with my head on the sewing machine where I've conked out and my head is marked with a dent from my head banging onto the machine. I do watch what equipment I am using, and some I will only use when someone else is there to supervise me. My goal is to have my own little business at home but I've got to get my episodes under some control before this will be able to start taking form, and I pray that I achieve this goal and I still have my ambitious side of me. That's keeping me going.

Living with my illnesses is very stressful for me, along with all my episodes. We have to plan everything. Some things need planning days in advance because it is not just me, it's also the person or persons who will be accompanying me.

My daily life became a life of daily seizures, conking out, blackouts, severe pain, memory loss, and spending day after day in bed, as that was the safest place for me. The pain I was in from my spine as it has gotten worse over the years, has become unbearable to the point where it causes me to have chest pains due to the muscles around my heart tensing and contracting when the pain flares up. This squeezes my heart so much that it feels like I'm having a heart attack. I have been rushed into hospital so many times that, at one point, for months our home life was spent with paramedics here with us on many occasions each week, scaring my kids each time when they had to call them out. I couldn't thank the paramedics enough, as they reassured my kids every time and made sure the kids saw me fully around before whisking me off to hospital, although on some occasions they had to take me straight away. My youngest was fourteen years old at this time, the second child was seventeen, and the eldest was nineteen. They were at ages that they could help me and understand what was going on.

We have an emergency alarm system in the home and I wear a bracelet or my pendant, so if I've got the bracelet on and I conk out and drop to the floor, or fall at any point it will trigger the alarm on impact, then someone will answer and speak to me or the kids through the box. If I'm at home alone and no one answers, they will then call my first contact and also the paramedics to come to my aid. The emergency services have access to my home so they can attend to me. It is very rare that I am left at home alone. The children always try their hardest to make sure someone is here to keep an eye on me. But if this is not so, then I will stay in bed. They will prepare food for me so the only thing I need to do is go to the bathroom. It is safest for me to stay in bed, because I will drop anywhere. They try not to leave me unattended for more than three to four hours maximum. I also have my pendant around my neck and mobile phone at hand just in case I get a warning first, then I can contact them and get one of them here straight away. They will also call every thirty to sixty minutes or text just to make sure all is well. If they receive a jumble up message back from me, then they know I'm having or have had an episode.

Food is prepared for me by others and we also buy pre-packed salads. All I need to do is get one out the fridge, and I don't have to use the microwave. I don't walk around the house with hot drinks in my hands. There've been numerous occasions when I was walking from the kitchen to the living room with a cup of tea or coffee and I collapsed to the floor, spilling the hot drink all over me. So, I don't walk around with them, someone else will transport it for me.

I have to be reminded about a lot of things, especially things like making sure all the bills are paid and having enough money to pay them. My medication is set up ready in pill boxes for each day. This way I have one box a day, and I'm monitored as to whether I've remembered to take them. This has worked great for me and is easy for my kids to keep on top of.

I don't go out on my own. I have someone with me to take care of me if anything happens and for vulnerability reasons. These are just some of my daily challenges. The biggest challenge is not being able to do the things I took for granted, thinking I would be able to do them for the rest of my life. Little did I realize that wasn't so.

*

CARRIE WORTHINGTON
Carrie was diagnosed with depression,
anxiety, and trichotillomania in 2000 at age 41

Prior to my husband's passing, and before my surgery, my depression was very bad. I was highly functioning in the business world, as well as at the nonprofit I led, but things at home were a disaster. I did not deal with the fact that both my son and husband went off their meds. My husband and I were not communicating, we had stopped our ritual of Saturday morning coffee, and I pretty much stayed oblivious to what was going on.

The hardest part for my anxiety and depression for the past few years has been being alone in my house. Three years ago, for the first time in my life, I was living alone. I used to feel very alone and the quiet in the house seemed very loud. When I had challenges at home to accomplish (house repair, etc.), it would at times cause anxiety, frustration and sadness, a feeling that I was alone. After having someone for twenty-three years to take care of me and the home, it was a huge adjustment, and throughout that adjustment there were many bouts of anxiety and/or depression. It has taken over four years of therapy for me to start looking at my accomplishments in a different way. Instead of immediately thinking I'm alone and have to handle this, I now think, "Look what I just did. Good job!" Shifting my focus has been a long difficult process for me. I have started to be successful at trying to focus on the good. If the negative thoughts surface, I'm more aware now and try to switch them, although it is still very new for me to hear the negative thinking and be aware of it, let it go, and try to go to a positive place instead.

*

Mental illness is a disorder, not a decision.
-ANONYMOUS

\*

CHAPTER TEN

# Our Functional Status

The secret of your future is hidden in your daily routine. -MIKE MURDOCK

Our routine activities of daily living include self-care, homemaking, work, and leisure. Health professionals routinely refer to our ability to perform these daily activities as a measure of our functional status. Does your mental illness prevent you from engaging in routine activities such as grocery shopping, driving a car, engaging in a career, or having a family?

*

ADRIANNE ALLEN-LANG
Adrianne was diagnosed with dissociative
identity disorder in 2015 at age 18

My mental illness does not prevent me from routine activities but it sure as heck makes it a thousand times harder. I get very short tempered and easily frustrated with my child. Just cooking a meal can take half a day's energy, and I don't have the capacity to get up and run about and play with him like he wants me to. It makes me feel like a useless mother some days, but I just try to remind myself I'm doing the absolute best I can and that's all anyone ever can do.

\*

MORGAN BUTLER
Morgan was diagnosed with depression
and anxiety in 2009 at age 15

Sometimes, I am scared to drive home from work. I get very anxious about what can go wrong on the road while I'm commuting, and sometimes while driving I even picture crashing into oncoming traffic, etc. When this happens, I try to call someone on the Bluetooth, or change the radio station to something I can sing along to. This distracts me enough to calm down and change my mindset.

Sometimes, I have issues being in crowds. On those days, I either try to make my trip as short and quick as possible (like getting groceries), or if I feel that this is too much of a trigger, I wait another day to do those errands.

I think that the biggest thing that helps me is communicating how I'm feeling to who I'm with. For example, my boyfriend and I grocery shop together a lot. Therefore, if I'm having a hard time thinking about going out and doing errands with him that day, I will communicate it with him. And either he will be gracious enough to do so without me, or sometimes he will think up a way to expedite our errands, or help me calm down before going. No matter what, I need to recognize that it's my mental illness, and that I can overcome it in that moment to accomplish even simple tasks. It's hard, and it's something that I deal with more frequently than I'd care to admit, but on at least two out of three of these days, it's mind over matter now.

\*

LYNDA CHELDELIN FELL
Lynda was diagnosed with depression in 2000 at age 35
and posttraumatic stress disorder in 2012 at age 47

My depression and PTSD don't prevent me from engaging in routine activities of daily living, though it did at one point. Now I'm careful and heed the warning symptoms of a depressive episode, because if left untreated it will lead to a complete mental shutdown.

One of my warning symptoms is loss of motivation. I'm normally highly motivated, and juggle many balls in the air with high efficiency. When my motivation wanes, I'm on red alert, ready to react to a possible depressive storm brewing on the horizon. The reason I'm so cautious is because once it gains a foothold, it's much harder to bring it under control. It does me no good to bury my head in the sand in hopes that it will go away. I already take excellent care of myself, I've already turned over all the stones I can to keep depression at bay. I know my symptoms, and I listen to them.

\*

SHAUNA COX
Shauna was diagnosed with an
anxiety disorder in 2009 at age 26

Certain routine activities like grocery shopping used to be especially difficult for me, and I refused to go at all without my husband. When we were at the store, I would make sure I had our car keys in my hand so that if I started to feel panicky, I could make a quick escape to the car. The thing is, as soon as I had those panicky feelings and left the store, I would suddenly feel better. I would go to the car anyway, and sit there thinking to myself that clearly if I felt better as soon as I left the building, the feelings were in my head. I would say this again and again to myself, take some deep breaths, and then make my way back into the store to find my husband and continue shopping. When in line, the panicky feelings would inevitably rush back, and I'd say to Roger, "I have to go," and walk quickly out of the store to the safety of our car. Back when the anxiety was really bad, I was upset that I couldn't manage to go to the store on my own. I worried about what would happen if Roger had to be away for work and I needed to get something. I knew how silly it all seemed, but even knowing that these feelings were all in my mind, it was a hard thing to fight.

Today, thanks to cognitive behavioral therapy (helped along with medication), I am proud to say that I can go shopping on my own. I never thought that would be something to be proud of, but looking back at how difficult that simple task was for me for a while, I am truly happy with myself for getting back to the point of independence. There are still moments when I go on my own and I feel a wave of anxiety rush over me, but I am generally good at listening to my inner voice to calm me down. I tell myself that it's in my head, and remind myself that I will be okay. I remember that if I am okay as soon as I leave the building, I will be okay to survive the rest of the trip without making a run for it.

*

JANE MCDONALD<br>
Jane was diagnosed with major depressive disorder in 1989,<br>
multiple anxiety disorders in 2001, multiple personality<br>
disorders in 2007, and dissociative identity disorder in 2014

Many routine activities are a struggle for me as a result of my various mental illnesses. Grocery shopping is highly anxiety provoking because of the crowds, the noise, the stress of trying to find items and having no one to help me, and the fear that another of my personalities will emerge and will be noticed or will do or say something inappropriate. This same type of anxiety prevents me from getting my driver's license. I feel a great deal of shame for not being able to do what, for most people without mental illness, are routine tasks. Worse still is that people who I tell that I have difficulty doing these things never understand why and tend to judge and criticize me, telling me to just do it or to suck it up and get these things done. They shame me for being unable to do what other people can do.

Engaging in a career has also been extremely difficult. I have many qualifications, but unfortunately have been burned out or fired from my jobs because of depression and anxiety. I have felt it necessary to keep my mental illness a secret at most workplaces due to fear of being penalized. Those employers who I've told about my depression and anxiety have been unwilling to accommodate me, and fired me when I got burned out or too anxious to work, rather than trying to work with me around my challenges.

I think many employers still prefer to fire someone with a mental illness who may be struggling, and simply hire someone else without any such difficulties. They simply don't want to invest the time or effort into helping us. This is another cause of great shame for me, that I can't be "normal." It also makes me frustrated and angry that society tells us that we are unable to contribute in the same way as people without mental illness. Where I live, many employers refuse to hire people with mental illnesses (although this is improving lately), and yet argue that we should not be able to receive unemployment benefits or social assistance because we cannot work.

Having a family was always something I wanted to do, and was expected to do. I always worried that I was getting too old to find someone and start a family with them. I worried about having a child, because many of the psychiatric medications that I depend on to function would harm an unborn child. I also experienced a great deal of fear that I would pass my mental illness on to my children, either through my genes or because I would be an inadequate mother. I have had great difficulty maintaining romantic relationships and know that this is true of many people with mental illness in general, particularly those with borderline personality disorder. I'm single and have no plans to enter into a romantic relationship. I know that I will never have children now, and have accepted that but it still makes me sad. I've always loved children and dreamed of one day fulfilling my family's tradition of having twins. I think it is a huge disappointment to my parents, my father in particular, that I will not make them grandparents. However, I know that I have to do what is best for me. Sadly, that doesn't include starting a family.

*

AMY OWEN
Amy was diagnosed with ADD and
bipolar disorder in 2014 at age 42

I avoid grocery shopping as much as possible, and when I do go, I rush through to get out. I am a nervous driver. I feel like people are staring at me and are mad about how I drive. I couldn't keep a job until now. It took a long time to feel like I could do it. I missed work a lot and was very unorganized. My boss told me that if I worked on this, they would keep me because I was good at what I did. I almost lost my family and that nearly killed me. I'll never let that happen again. I work hard at staying in the moment and spending quality time with them. Plus I now have rules and show them how to be good adults.

\*

DENISE PURCELL
Denise was diagnosed with depression, posttraumatic stress
disorder, and dissociative identity disorder in 1995 at age 30

Yes and no. I can do some, but only on a good day or if I have to. I find being around people sometimes gives me anxiety attacks. Having a family, not so much, because my girls are either out of the house or at college. I will chat when I can, but I'm very good at presenting the mask I need at any given moment. I only drive when I feel safe enough to drive if my seizures that are part of my mental illness won't affect me, but sometimes it's a coin toss. Sometimes I don't care if anything happens to me. There have been times while going into surgery that I wouldn't mind if I didn't wake up. I know that sounds bad. It's not about really doing it, it's about how bad I feel.

\*

ERICKA REEVE
Ericka was diagnosed with dissociative identity disorder,
posttraumatic stress disorder, obsessive-compulsive disorder,
depression, anxiety and an eating disorder in 2013 at age 26

At times yes, of course it does. How could so many varying illnesses and problematic contradictory things, not prevent things at times? A few years ago after a few months of a blackout, I came to find that our therapist had suggested we not drive for a while. Before I knew why I was blacking out, my parts whom are legally and very capable of driving, would go somewhere and then pull to the roadside where I would then "come back." This got confusing and troublesome, and as such, we tend to err on the side of caution; it's who we are. We discussed this with our doctor and decided it best that we wait until we were a more stabilized system before driving.

I'm also a type one diabetic. With so much chaos and switching going on, it was affecting my blood sugar. I don't ever operate a vehicle of any kind without testing my blood sugar. This is true for my parts as well, we will not allow someone to be accidentally harmed at our hands. We refuse, when we can prevent this.

As for my career, it has fizzled and now changed directions. Due to my now severely limiting physical and mental illnesses, I can no longer work. I have not in several years now, but we are working on things and making an attempt to find some sort of income.

Without working, when we got married, I lost my insurance; something that yet again caused chaos. It is a major struggle fighting to constantly get the medications you very much need to survive. Not to live comfortably, mind you, but to survive. I'm tired of surviving. We very much want to be able to live one day.

*

LORRAINE SCOTT
Lorraine was diagnosed with non-epilepsy attack disorder
and dissociative identity disorder in 2016 at age 48

I have tried my hardest to keep my independence in the home. There have been times when I would try to cook but I would start putting stuff together, put pans on the cooker ring (gas ones), and I would totally forget all about them. I wouldn't realize until someone smelled burning or the fire alarms would go off. By this time, I've already conked out and have no knowledge of what I've done and the risk I'm putting my kids in. So, it was best that I didn't cook or even go into the kitchen, and so they banned me from the kitchen. This wasn't all that went on in the kitchen, there was much more. For instance, I had my arm over a naked flame from stirring a pan on the flame behind. I had an absence seizure and my sleeve caught on fire. Lucky for me, my kitchen is medium to small in size so it was just a quick turn to the sink to put out the flames. This could have been devastating for us all.

I've left the tap running in the sink; I've poured boiling water into a cup and stood there not realizing the boiling water is overflowing down my clothes scorching my thighs; I've scalded my hands, thinking I was putting them into cold water when I hadn't poured the boiling water away; I've pulled trays out of the hot oven with my naked hands; I've used the microwave and put food that has been over heated into my mouth and burned it numerous times.

This is all due to me having absence seizures and my mind as losing what it was doing in the first place, hence the reason it's not safe for me to be in the kitchen. I do try and assist or tell the kids how to cook certain foods that I can remember. Considering I used to cook up some wonderful meals and bake some gorgeous cakes and cupcakes, I couldn't stand and do that now. My brain feels like it's been scrambled and everything at times is all jumbled up and confused as to where it belongs. As a strategy, I focus on very minimum things now and try to deal with one thing at a time instead of multitasking. Hopefully in time this will help to strengthen the function of my brain if I also try avoiding stress as much as I possibly can, and resting as much as I can.

The first thing that stripped me of independence was not being able to drive. It was very upsetting to see my car outside the window, yet I couldn't freely get in it and drive away because of the seizures, conking out, and blackouts. Years ago, before all of this became so severe, I was unaware of what was going on and I'd be driving and not know how I got from point A to point B. I had been having total blackouts for years and was completely unaware until I consulted with my doctor about this. Straight away, he said I was no longer allowed to drive and stopped me from driving. I was gutted, but this was for my safety and the safety of others, so I wasn't going to risk hurting anyone. Lives are far more important than driving a car. So, in a way I was happy to stop driving immediately as this took some stresses away from me. However, it is so strange and frustrating having to rely and wait around for others, and seven years later, I still get frustrated. My day became planned around others and what they were able to do to help me throughout each day, taking into consideration that they all have their own lives and families and work too, so most of this fell on my children and partner at the time. My children knew that they could reach out to others if needed, so they weren't alone in this. I was also attending a lot of medical appointments that someone had to take me to and be able to speak for me when necessary.

I have, however, been very fortunate to have married and have a family. Although my marriage broke down after twelve years of being together, we had three stunning children and now have three stunning grandchildren too. This shows that having mental illnesses doesn't mean you can't live a normal life. It has not prevented me from being a wife or girlfriend, mother, grandmother, sister, aunty, niece, cousin, or a trusting genuine friend. Some members of my family are aware of my illnesses, some I've only told that I have seizures and the effect that it has on me, but only speak of it if it's going to prevent me from attending a function. My close friends know about my illnesses too. Neither friends nor family, the close genuine ones anyway, treat me any different than normal except for showing their concerns for me, and that they love and care for me. They treat me the same as the person they grew up with or have known at some point in their lives.

I'm still the same person I have been for the last fifty years, the only difference is that I've matured, I'm a lot wiser, I appreciate all those around me for all that they do, and I never take anyone or thing for granted. I have blackouts, seizures, conk out, have memory loss, and switch personalities, but my brain still functions normally. I can hold intelligent intellectual conversations, I have fun, and I do most things that everyone else does mentally.

Imagine that your computer has been running for a long time without a break and it starts to freeze up, then it starts automatically shutting down. You then reboot it and it runs okay for a short time but then keeps doing the same over and over again. As the memory gets more full, it starts to run slower and slower, freezing more and constantly shutting down, rebooting, etc. In addition, you need antivirus and theft protection while browsing the web. Well, that's just how the brain works. It's like a living, working computer and that's what happens with my brain. It freezes, shuts down, reboots itself, in addition to having many different protections against harm. I think this is pretty cool and not a bad thing at all.

Physically it is different for me because I am restricted, but I haven't given up.

I do try to go shopping, but for the past seven to eight years it's been once every couple of months. There was one point where I couldn't do it at all, I was too scared to go out because of the seizures and having people stare at me if I were to have one while out. Back then, they were happening no matter what I was doing and we didn't see any pattern, and so I couldn't work out what I could and couldn't do. It's taken us a good five to six years to find a pattern and what the triggers are so we can now prepare for them. I have periods where I can go out at least once or twice a week, sometimes more, but the more I go and do things, the more seizures I will have. It's the same around the house too.

When I do go out shopping, we have to take the wheelchair. Sometimes I will walk and suffer in pain just to get some exercise. Although this is good for the brain as well as the body, it is extremely painful for me and will shorten the length of time I can be out. Unfortunately I can no longer work because:

- I am high risk
- I need someone constantly with me
- I have uncontrolled seizures
- I have blackouts and memory loss
- I am unable to retain information
- I'm in severe pain
- How vulnerable I am puts others at risk

The last company I worked for did their best to accommodate me, but things got worse with the conking out and blackouts. When the seizures started and I became high risk, they terminated my contract. My illness has worsened since then, and I'm now unemployable. This doesn't mean it's the end of the world. I have goals and hopefully in time or years to come, I will reach them.

*

CARRIE WORTHINGTON
Carrie was diagnosed with depression,
anxiety, and trichotillomania in 2000 at age 41

For over a year after my husband passed, I was angry when I had to do all the routine activities like laundry, grocery shopping, going to the gas station, etc. This is something I did not have to do for twenty-three years and I knew I was doing it because he wasn't here. I would wait to do these things until I just didn't have a choice but to do what I needed to do. I no longer feel angry, but there are things I still push back on. I have also avoided socializing when I was feeling down, which I know cognitively would be the one thing that would really help the feeling of loneliness. I believe those around me are now aware that sometimes I just can't socialize. This happens very rarely now. I have really tried to push my limits, step out of my comfort zone, and experience and do things that I have always wanted to do.

Facing mundane, routine things as well as new adventures will, for a moment, cause a brief wave of grief. Nowadays, however, it is very brief and I usually don't lose momentum. There are times when I might need a day or two to myself to regroup because of job stress or something else. But this is usually not isolating, it's just giving myself quiet time. I don't feel bad about having to do this, because it's an important part of taking care of myself, and I recognize that sometimes I just need to recharge.

*

LIVING WITH MENTAL ILLNESS

There's something about being broken
at various times in your life that makes
you a more complete person.

J. IRON WOOD
*

# CHAPTER ELEVEN

# Exploring Therapy Options

I'm on a constant path of self-discovery and change. I'm trying to become a better person, a nicer person. I love therapy—it's brilliant. -JULIA SAWALHA

When it comes to mental illness and treatment, there is no such thing as one size fits all. Some find medication effective on its own. Others find medication combined with psychotherapy to be a better combination. How do you feel about therapy? Do you find it helpful?

\*

ADRIANNE ALLEN-LANG
Adrianne was diagnosed with dissociative
identity disorder in 2015 at age 18

Because of the mixture of my issues, most therapists find us too complex and difficult to deal with. I find dialectical behavior therapy extremely helpful, but generalized therapy not so much. It helps me to be able to debrief on my emotions and weekly stresses but unless I'm having intense trauma recovery therapy, it's not that useful.

\*

MORGAN BUTLER
Morgan was diagnosed with depression
and anxiety in 2009 at age 15

I believe that treatment is the first step of admitting it to yourself and realizing the significance of living with mental illness. Some people work best with medication, some counseling and other forms of therapy, and all of those things are okay. For me personally, because of my family's history of issues with chemical dependency, I avoided medication at all costs. However, I did undergo cognitive behavioral therapy to learn better ways to recognize my triggers and learn coping mechanisms that worked for me.

I have not been to treatment since 2010, but am now much more open about how I'm feeling and try to communicate when I'm in a low or having an anxiety attack.

\*

LYNDA CHELDELIN FELL
Lynda was diagnosed with depression in 2000 at age 35
and posttraumatic stress disorder in 2012 at age 47

In 2014, I wrote an article about an experience with a therapist who was of no help. While it was written about grief, the counseling situation can be applied to anything. Just like any profession, there are good therapists and bad therapists. If one doesn't fit your style, find another. Following is the excerpt.

"Well, no, I don't specialize in grief specifically but with my many years of experience, I'm confident I can help you," said the counselor on the other end of the phone. It had been eighteen months since we lost our teenage daughter in a car accident, and my husband and I were caught in the black abyss of sadness and hopelessness. We were finally ready to wave the white flag and seek help.

Many well-meaning family and friends urged us to get counseling immediately after the accident, but I adamantly refused. I bristled at the very idea that someone would tell me how to grieve the loss of my beloved child. Worse, there was no way I wanted to be trapped in a group of crying mothers stuck in their own horrible grief. No, I would rather do it myself, for I didn't want to be part of that club in the first place.

But over the coming months as reality sank in and the nightmare became permanent, we found ourselves on autopilot, barely staying afloat on the outside and dead on the inside. By design, men and women are wired differently. So as husband and wife, we were each caught in our own despair. We had nothing left to give each other, let alone our marriage.

By the time we realized we needed help processing our grief, we had fallen so deep into the black abyss that even the simple task of finding a counselor felt utterly overwhelming. So I dug deep to muster what energy I could to google local counselors, and called the first number I saw.

And thus began an eighteen-month relationship with a counselor who knew absolutely nothing about grief. She was a lovely woman, and in looking back I'm sure she learned a great deal from us as her clients. But much to our dismay, we gained nothing from our appointments. At least we hadn't gone backwards, I told myself, but the idea of trying to find a better counselor was simply too overwhelming. So we stayed where we were, week after week for eighteen months.

And then tragedy struck once again. Three years after losing our daughter, my forty-six-year-old husband suffered a major stroke. He went from being a highly intelligent, well respected, vibrant man who managed multi-million dollar projects, to an invalid wearing a hospital gown in the intensive care unit. He couldn't walk, talk, read, or write. My beloved soul mate, my dear sweet husband, suffered a major embolic stroke in the left frontal lobe. Paralyzing the entire right side of his body, the damage also destroyed the region of his brain that controls communication. He understood those around him, but he couldn't speak at all. Nor could he read, write, or comprehend letters and numbers. We found ourselves facing a fresh, new black abyss, and we hadn't even found our way out of the first one.

And then help arrived in the form of a neuropsychologist who made daily hospital rounds to the stroke unit. His specialty was supporting patients facing significant disabilities and helping them adapt to a new way of life. Now that my husband was trapped in a hospital bed, he could no longer bury his grief in eighty-hour work weeks. The neuropsychologist found himself doubly tasked with not only helping us adjust to our new life left in the wake of my husband's stroke, but assisting us in processing the profound, unresolved grief left in the wake of our daughter's death.

Dr. Ford was in his early fifties, about the same age as our prior counselor. He was tall and fit, and his short hair yielded to a stubborn childhood cowlick he never outgrew. His face was kind, his voice calm yet intelligent. My husband and I liked him immediately. And, to our collective surprise, Dr. Ford's specialty of helping stroke patients face a new life with severe disabilities, wasn't all that different from helping the bereaved face a new life without their loved one. And thus began a professional relationship in which we finally found the help needed to process our double sorrow.

It has now been over three years since my husband's life-changing stroke, and six years since our daughter's passing. Because of the plasticity of the human brain and its ability to rewire around dead tissue, my husband continues to improve beyond medical expectation. Through intense inpatient and then dedicated outpatient rehabilitation, he learned to walk again and use his right hand though he still can't feel anything on his right side. His speech remains challenged, and he fatigues quite easily, preventing him from returning to gainful employment, and our family from returning to our former life.

We continue to see the neuropsychologist though the frequency changes depending upon our needs. As far as I see it, the life-changing stroke was actually a lifeline in disguise, for it brought a compassionate, intuitive, and highly skilled practitioner through the door of my husband's hospital room and into our lives. And although Dr. Ford came because of the devastating stroke, his counseling proved to be the help we desperately needed to navigate our daughter's death.

I am not angry we spent eighteen months with a counselor who was unable to meet our needs. Actually, I admire her for accepting us as clients in the first place. She didn't harm us, and she did try her best to help us, and I am forever thankful. But I wish I had acknowledged sooner just how critically important it is to find the right care in our darkest hours.

When one suffers a heart attack, they call in a cardiologist. When one has a broken leg, they call in an orthopedist. So when one faces profound loss, a highly skilled and qualified practitioner to help navigate the way through, and eventually out of, the deep abyss of overwhelming grief is just as crucial.

With over 168,000 counselors available in the U.S. alone, there is no shortage from which to choose. If your counselor is unable to help you navigate a life-changing loss or challenge, don't be afraid to find another. Just as grief isn't one size fits all, neither is support.

Can a heart attack patient survive without a cardiologist? Yes, but the chances of surviving and thriving are much greater when under the care of a proper practitioner. This applies to all wounds, including mental illness.

\*

SHAUNA COX
Shauna was diagnosed with an
anxiety disorder in 2009 at age 26

I find therapy to be very helpful. Unfortunately, it's also expensive and as a result I haven't been able to take advantage of it as much as I would like. When the anxiety was at its worst for me, I was going to a psychologist about once a month. I feel like it would have been more helpful had I been able to go weekly (which is what my therapist recommended), but financial concerns limited me in that respect.

There were two psychologists that I was going to when the anxiety was at its peak. The first one I had to stop going to due to a conflict of interest: my husband had started acting in a local dinner theater with my therapist, and as a result I had to switch psychologists. However, both of them were immensely supportive and helpful to me along my journey to healing. They helped me step outside of myself and consider some of my fears from a more objective point of view, which helped me see that a lot of my thoughts were unreasonable. I learned valuable strategies in therapy that have become part of my regular coping mechanism. My favorite strategy is to say this mantra to myself: "How it was in the past is not how it is now." It reminds me how far I've come, that the anxiety is a lot better now compared to how it was before, and because I'm better, I can get through the day and succeed.

I was also encouraged to say "the" anxiety as opposed to "my" anxiety to remind myself that the anxiety isn't who I am. I am separate from the anxiety; it is not attached to me and I can escape it. I also learned some calming techniques for when the anxiety was nearing a ten on a ten-point scale, and ways of letting go of some of the things I can't control in life.

While medication is a huge help as well, I don't think I would have progressed as far as I have today had it not been for cognitive behavioral therapy. It taught me life-changing strategies and got me to change my thinking enough that, even outside the walls of the therapist's office, I can take it with me into the real world and hopefully eventually, overcome this disorder completely!

\*

JANE MCDONALD
Jane was diagnosed with major depressive disorder in 1989,
multiple anxiety disorders in 2001, multiple personality
disorders in 2007, and dissociative identity disorder in 2014

After my first hospitalization for mental health, I was forced to participate in individual psychotherapy. I resented being there, did not like the therapist and did not feel she understood me. I was also put into group therapy where I was the last person to join the group, and subsequently felt like the new person throughout the rest of group and I didn't get much out of that either. Since then, I have seen a number of different therapists and participated in different types of therapies, ranging from dialectical behavioral therapy to cognitive behavioral therapy, psychoanalytic, and hypnotherapy to a more eclectic approach. I have found each technique to have their own strengths and weaknesses but it wasn't until recently that I felt I was getting much out of therapy.

It wasn't until I entered group therapy based on the principles of dialectical behavior therapy and psychoeducation that I started to feel I was gaining anything from the time I spent with therapists. Prior to this, I found that the approach adopted by my therapists was one of crisis management: addressing whatever crisis or conflict had arisen in the past week, but never focusing on longer-term issues or developing lasting coping skills. I went, I would talk, they would listen. I didn't feel I was getting anywhere or accomplishing anything.

Even short-term goals of returning to school, forming lasting and meaningful relationships, even basic self-care goals always fell to the wayside as they focused on whatever was happening in that exact moment. I know that this is often a difficult balance to find, particularly for those of us with borderline personality disorder, as there always seems to be a crisis. However, it is imperative that therapists see beyond the immediate moment and focus on longer-term solutions. It is so important not only to be reactive, but also to be proactive. It was this proactive element that I always felt was lacking. It was only as I entered dialectical behavioral therapy that I started to learn actual strategies to manage my emotions, to deal with crises, but also to focus on actually developing skills to prevent moments of crisis. Crises will always exist in my life, but I can't just focus on those.

Unfortunately, the people who were teaching me dialectical behavioral therapy were very hostile and not willing to have their methods or what they said questioned by anyone, particularly (it felt) by me. They were the experts and we were to blindly follow and do whatever they said to do, whether it was feasible or not. One of the leaders in my DBT group actually told a friend of mine that if she did not directly and firmly say "no" to a male who was pursuing her (which she was not able to do because of lack of self-confidence and other reasons), that she was literally "asking for it," meaning she was asking to be raped. I brought up this concern as did others in the group but we were shot down and dismissed. To have someone teaching a group full of women with personality disorders (many of whom have been sexually assaulted or raped) who believes that a woman, under any circumstance, is "asking for it" and deserves to be raped is not helpful and can be extremely harmful. As a result, I didn't feel that I derived as much benefit from this form of therapy as I could have if they had had a different set of leaders.

Other things that have not worked have been therapists who, at the slightest hint of feelings of suicide or self-harm, threaten to hospitalize you or even call the police. I need to feel safe and develop a sense of trust with my therapist. Threatening hospitalization (which is NOT advised for individuals with borderline personality disorder, such as myself) ruins any progress or trust that may have already existed. If there is no trust, the relationship between therapist and client will suffer. This has been the case with almost all of my past therapists.

Fortunately, my current psychiatrist and I have an understanding that hospitalization is not an option. We make other arrangements and agree that I will not self-harm, and we try to work on the underlying causes in a proactive way during therapy.

I've also had issues with psychiatrists relying too heavily on medication. I admit that medication plays an important role in my treatment, but I don't agree that it should be the entirety of what is done. Unfortunately, my previous psychiatrist relied too heavily on meds, and medicated me for conditions I didn't have. When I switched psychiatrists, my new one said I was one of the most overmedicated patients he had ever treated.

I am fortunate enough to now have an amazing psychiatrist. He is kind, compassionate and caring. He is a great listener, but also makes practical suggestions on how to deal with particular issues that come up. He is excellent at challenging the way I think about circumstances, and making me see things in a more helpful, beneficial light. He prescribes medication, but it is manageable and not numbing the way the other medications had been. For once, I feel that I'm genuinely benefiting from therapy. I only wish it hadn't taken me so long to find a therapist I could work with and benefit from.

*

AMY OWEN
Amy was diagnosed with ADD and
bipolar disorder in 2014 at age 42

I find the medication very, very helpful. I find therapy helpful but hard to go to. It is difficult to talk about things that I'm embarrassed about, ashamed of and mostly the things that hurt the ones I love. I feel like I'm going to break apart from pain and shame.

\*

DENISE PURCELL
Denise was diagnosed with depression, posttraumatic stress
disorder, and dissociative identity disorder in 1995 at age 30

Not really. I go with the intention of hope. And it's a place where
they know what I have so it's not very awkward, and for an hour, if
nothing else, I can socialize or pick their brains. I wish therapists did
understand better. They go by what they were taught, even if the
patient is right, they're telling them differently. Guidelines are just
that: to guide. Not define. Not everything needs to be taken care of
with medication. That numbs, it does not help.

\*

ERICKA REEVE
Ericka was diagnosed with dissociative identity disorder,
posttraumatic stress disorder, obsessive-compulsive disorder,
depression, anxiety and an eating disorder in 2013 at age 26

Yes! More than you could ever know. It is hard at times, most of
the time, but I know for me that means it's being effective. It is helpful
because I've finally got the answers I needed to know what was
happening in my life.

Someone praying is a thoughtful sentiment, I guess, but I wanted
to actually do something and have something be done for the
problems that were occurring. Prayer is a wishful thinking action,
while seeing a therapist is helpful.

At this point in therapy, I really don't think there is something we
wish she could better understand. She knows us well, and is
continually getting to know others, but when something challenging
comes up, we discuss it and work through it together.

\*

LORRAINE SCOTT
Lorraine was diagnosed with non-epilepsy attack disorder
and dissociative identity disorder in 2016 at age 48

I recommend therapy to anyone if it's readily available for them. I attended a local therapy group for those of us who suffer with non-epileptic attack disorder. This was great for group learning, coping strategies, understanding what NEAD is, and how to live with this disorder. It was nice to actually see that there were others who had this illness. Group therapy took away the lonely feeling I had, and the feeling that no one understood really what I was going through.

There was also the feeling that people thought you were making it up. When I was first diagnosed, I had heard the name only a few times before, and that was through my neurologist. After researching it, I could see why they felt that I may have this. It took five years to be diagnosed with this illness, so you can imagine I was relieved to see others and talk to people who truly understood this debilitating illness that I was experiencing and had taken over my life. It isn't nice for anyone to have any form of illness, but unfortunately we do. It's difficult and lonely when having a long-term illness, as people give up on you, they forget, and before you know it you're on your own. So, any form of therapy is wise because illness, especially long term ones, can breed more illness.

I found this particular therapy to be very interesting, therapeutic and helpful. We were taught relaxation techniques and how to understand triggers. Although we may have different triggers from other people, we were given handouts containing plenty of information that was useful to everyone. We had to keep track of our seizures and log one per day so we could see if there was a pattern and work out some of our own triggers, strategies to slow the build up to a seizure down, and given websites to look at and music for relaxation. Each week, we had to do something nice and treat ourselves to something from a cup of coffee, or a slice of cake, to something we've been wanting or saving for. One of my biggest treats was a Brother sewing and quilting machine; that was the grand finale of my closing session. This was a treat because I had lost so much and gone through so much over the past seven years. This was a "well done" present for not giving up on myself. I treated myself to a yard or two of fabric, or out for lunch, or days out shopping. We could do anything we wanted as this was all about us and no one else. Every month, I would treat myself to something big or small, it didn't matter as long as it made me smile and made me feel that I had achieved something good that month. Having happy thoughts helps you feel better about yourself.

The only downside to the therapy, and it wasn't the therapy itself, was that I had to travel forty miles to get to that specific hospital, but it was all well worth it. It became a day out for me and the kids and it gave us more quality time together, and they were happy that they were helping mom to get better just by taking me there.

After each therapy session, I was always happier than I'd been the previous days leading up to therapy day. The kids and I continued going out once a week for meals, shopping and doing other stuff. They knew that they needed to get me out of the house at least once a week, as they saw a big difference in my moods when I was out. I really enjoyed this and we continue to do it still, although some weeks it can't happen, but I always look forward to the next time. Those therapy sessions were great and I wished they never had to end, but I came away a different person than when I started the sessions.

I've just started a road to recovery course, which is another group session preparing us all for our individual one-on-one therapy. I didn't realize how difficult and how long it takes to get therapy through the mental health team. Something really needs to be done about that, because it's so unfair to all those people out there that need therapy and may have to wait two years before getting any. Some people are not in a good state of mind, and waiting months or years for therapy could be too late for them. I don't believe that people who are in need of immediate therapy should have to be put on a waiting list. I've seen people who need urgent therapy and they are still waiting, just as I have been, for twelve months and still not getting one-on-one therapy. This is so bad, and shows that something needs to be done about this as soon as possible.

In some cases, I don't agree with group therapy, especially when it's dealing with a group of people who have all had a traumatic life from childhood through to adulthood. The reason being is that someone else could be informing the group about the traumas they have gone through, and without their knowledge of the traumas that others in the group have been through or still going through, they could be triggering off traumatic memories for them. Now I've experienced this and I wanted to get up and walk out, I felt so uncomfortable, emotional and totally shocked. I was horrified of the things that were being said, but the other person hadn't been told to be careful with the information they give as this could be a trigger to others. I can understand one wanting to tell all, but a warning should have been given to the group first. This in itself was traumatic to hear, and I cried and cried for days after. This brought me back down after spending months trying to get out of the very dark place I was in.

However, I will still advise anyone in need of help to seek therapy if it's offered. If it isn't offered, then ask for it and keep asking your doctor for it. Don't give up.

*

CARRIE WORTHINGTON
Carrie was diagnosed with depression,
anxiety, and trichotillomania in 2000 at age 41

I believe therapy has helped me quite a bit. It has helped me recognize how I react to things, my thought patterns and how to start working on seeing things in a better and different way. I have lived for a long time not looking at how and why I was reacting to things. I am aware of how my mind goes to self-defeating thoughts, and if I dwell, it gets worse. I have recognized the self-deprecating thoughts that used to bring me to low points. I have been able to recognize the thoughts and I have learned what to do to turn those around. My therapist has been kind and patient. I sometimes wonder if he is bored and gets frustrated as some things that I still talk about are the same things I have talked about for four years. I think even I'm bored with it. I am so grateful that he has been my doctor, especially when the times were really bad. He would steer me in the right directions, giving me the tools to handle the changes and things that were happening in my life. I have become more aware in general, sometimes I can make it better, sometimes I can't and it becomes the subject of the next visit. With these years of therapy and the proper medication, I do believe I am now in a place that is healthier, mentally, than I have ever been in.

*

People who need help sometimes look
a lot like people who don't need help.
GLENNON MELTON

*

# CHAPTER TWELVE

# Confessing Resentments

To find gratitude and generosity when you could reasonably find hurt and resentment will surprise you. -HENRY B. EYRING

When diagnosed with a mental illness, many feel resentment. After all, nobody wants to live with a mental illness. We're terrified of being shunned and alone. Real or imagined, our feelings are common. Do you ever feel resentment about living with mental illness?

\*

ADRIANNE ALLEN-LANG
Adrianne was diagnosed with dissociative
identity disorder in 2015 at age 18

I feel resentment, rage, envy, and sadness all the time. I just ignore it as I wouldn't wish this upon anyone. In a way, I pity those without mental illness, not for not having one, but for not being able to understand the good and the bad within someone with a mental illness. Too often just the negative side is focused on, and no one talks about the incredible things mentally ill people can often accomplish.

\*

MORGAN BUTLER
Morgan was diagnosed with depression
and anxiety in 2009 at age 15

Yes, I have had moments in my life when this has happened. For the most part, people who live without mental illness try to be sympathetic when I express my condition, and I recognize that they are trying to understand to the best of their ability and I cannot hold that against them. There have, however, been cases in the past when I have dated someone, or been close friends with someone, who didn't understand my mental illness to the point where it seemed like they lacked sympathy when I was in my lowest of lows. This did lead to resentment and unfortunately the end of my relationship or friendship with these people.

I've learned that most people have good intentions. The ones who cause that resentment because they aren't open enough to try to understand what I'm going through, those are people who are not healthy for me to surround myself with, at least in my inner circle. For me, cutting these ties has been difficult but extremely liberating in my journey to cope with depression and anxiety.

\*

LYNDA CHELDELIN FELL
Lynda was diagnosed with depression in 2000 at age 35
and posttraumatic stress disorder in 2012 at age 47

I don't feel resentment about living with a mental illness, though I can see how misunderstandings can easily lead to resentment on both sides. For those who don't share the path or understand the journey, I feel great compassion. How lucky are they to live without the stigma of a mental illness? They don't know what they don't know. When someone applies a judgment, stigma or an urban legend to a mental illness, it stings, yes. But I have compassion for those who judge things they don't understand, for it reveals a flaw in their own character. I personally know many who are flawed that way, but I have my own flaws, so I still love them, flaws and all.

\*

SHAUNA COX
Shauna was diagnosed with an
anxiety disorder in 2009 at age 26

I have never felt resentment toward others who don't live with a mental illness. If anything, I might have felt a bit jealous of people who are able to socialize with others without constantly second guessing themselves or overanalyzing everything, or of those who don't think twice if their spouse is late getting home from work rather than jumping to the worst-case scenario. I wonder sometimes why some people end up with a mental illness, and others don't, but I know that that's not the fault of anyone. Some people have better luck of the draw when it comes to sanity I guess!

The one thing that I sometimes have a hard time with are people who don't understand what I go through. I have experienced some hurtful comments surrounding my shyness and social anxiety from people who think they're making a joke, but I end up taking it to heart because I'm already overthinking every little thing as it is.

I also get upset when I hear someone say, "Why don't you just get over it already?" or "Why can't you just relax? It's not that hard to just let it go." It's hard for me to explain to people who don't understand that it's not like I'm not trying to let things go. It's as if my body and my mind won't cooperate. I want to let worries go. I want to be social and not stress about millions of things at once. It's like my mind is fighting with itself, and my body is either frozen in fear or fighting to get away. For those not struggling with mental illness, it can be hard to truly understand what it's like, and I get upset at people who think it's easier to deal with than it is. Mental illness is a struggle. No matter what diagnosis a person has, it is a fight, and what might seem easy to someone without mental illness is Mount Everest to climb for someone who lives with one.

*

JANE MCDONALD
Jane was diagnosed with major depressive disorder in 1989,
multiple anxiety disorders in 2001, multiple personality
disorders in 2007, and dissociative identity disorder in 2014

For those of us who live with mental illness every day, it can be difficult at times to not feel some form of resentment toward those who don't. This can be particularly hard on the darkest days when even getting out of bed is a challenge. It's hard not to feel an inkling of jealousy toward those who don't have depression, who have never had a panic attack, or who don't struggle with the things I do. On these days, I try to remind myself of a quote that I read a while ago: everyone you meet is fighting a battle you know nothing about.

As someone with an invisible illness (mental illness), I need to remind myself that many others have mental, physical or spiritual struggles that aren't readily apparent but are equally as difficult. I know nothing about the challenges of living with cancer, lupus, diabetes, or with loss of hearing or sight. Their days, I am sure, are just as full of challenges as my own. They face obstacles too, and while they're different than my own, they're no less valid or difficult.

Although I make a conscious effort to not resent people without mental illness, there are things about them that I often do resent. I resent, at times, their ignorance of what life is like with mental illness, about how hard things are for those of us who live with psychiatric disorders. I resent the comments that well-meaning people make, like "Snap out of it," or "Change your thinking," or "You're not even trying," or "It's your choice to be depressed," or other insensitive things such as this.

I wish people would understand and view mental illness as they would any other physical illness. It is not something we choose, it's not something we can snap out of, or wish away with positive thinking. There is often a biochemical basis to these illnesses that we can treat with medications, but there is more to it than that.

I also resent the stigma and the stereotypes that exist. I resent that people tell us we are faking it or doing it for attention. Although I would never, ever wish mental illness upon anyone, I do wish they could experience just a hint of how life is when you have depression, anxiety, bipolar disorder, schizophrenia, dissociative identity disorder, or any other mental illness.

*

AMY OWEN
Amy was diagnosed with ADD and
bipolar disorder in 2014 at age 42

I wish they would try to have some understanding, but I think they are lucky. I want them to see how lucky they are and help or care about those of us who do have these issues.

*

DENISE PURCELL
Denise was diagnosed with depression, posttraumatic stress
disorder, and dissociative identity disorder in 1995 at age 30

No, I really don't. It's not their fault they don't have a mental
illness and it's not mine. I wish there were less biased opinions of
mental illness. For example, if someone does something out of
character, the word "mental" is used. Criminals are thought to be
mentally unstable. That might be so, but not all of them. And they
have a choice. There is always a choice.

*

ERICKA REEVE
Ericka was diagnosed with dissociative identity disorder,
posttraumatic stress disorder, obsessive-compulsive disorder,
depression, anxiety and an eating disorder in 2013 at age 26

No. Why would I? There is no logic in that. Sure, from my
perspective their lives may seem easier in some way or another, but
they have problems I do not. Everyone struggles at times and
comparing myself to other people, when we've lived immensely
different lives, does not make any logical sense to me.

*

LORRAINE SCOTT
Lorraine was diagnosed with non-epilepsy attack disorder
and dissociative identity disorder in 2016 at age 48

I've spent my life thinking that I would never resent anyone but
that is so not true, I've spent my life resenting others for the bad things
that they have done to me. I've never thought about people without
mental illness because I've gone forty-five out of fifty years where I've
had mental illness. I didn't know until 2016, so I've gone all my life like

this, thinking I wasn't living with mental illnesses. How far from the truth was I? I've stored all the bad that has happened to me somewhere in my brain, thinking that it's locked away and won't ever surface again, but the truth is each time I think or see someone or something that is a reminder, the resentment is fed again.

There is one person I know now that I do resent, and that is due to the fact that when I was diagnosed with DID, he abandoned me. This person has caused me a lot of pain, upset, unhappiness, loss of confidence, feelings of betrayal, of being unwanted, not good enough, of no self-esteem, I feel ugly and unattractive, he has broken my heart. So when I looked up the word resentment this is some of what I found:

To feel angry because you have been forced to accept someone or something that you do not like. The strong and painful bitterness you feel when someone does something wrong to you doesn't have actual physical weight, but it feels very heavy and can last a long time. It's a feeling of anger because something has happened that you think is unfair. Bitterness, indignation, irritation, displeasure, dissatisfaction, disgruntlement, discontentment, discontent, resentfulness, bad feelings, hard feelings, ill feelings, acrimony, rancor, animosity, hostility, jaundice, antipathy, antagonism, enmity, hatred, hate.

The psychological meaning of resentment is a negative emotional state that combines annoyance, anger, dislike or hatred, and other negative feelings that interferes with a person's ability to relate to another person or situation. This emotional state is often hidden or repressed to allow a person to continue to function as needed.

Resentment refers to the mental process of repetitively replaying a feeling, and the events leading up to it, that goads or angers us.

How many of us can relate to some of these? I found that a lot of these words describe how I've felt throughout my life, also within the last twelve months with going through a breakup and divorce, having to move out of my home temporarily due to water damage, and being diagnosed with a mental illness. I never realized how much resentment I have actually been storing. Here are just some of how I can relate to some of these words.

Hating the fact that I felt unwanted my whole life.

Bitterness for not having my father in my life as a child.

Hurt because I felt that my mother didn't like me.

Discontentment in the length of time it took to be diagnosed.

Indignation toward those who bullied me.

Animosity toward those who hurt me mentally, physically and emotionally, let me down, lied to me and abandoned me in my time of need.

Dissatisfaction because I lost my job and independence.

Antipathy because of the things I saw when I was a child.

These are just some that have stirred to the forefront, I was unaware that I even had these emotions in me. I spent my whole life hiding the truth behind the face of Lorraine, behind the smile was and is a world of pain and torture that no one would ever dream was going on. I've always felt from a young age that I wanted to make people feel better and that was because I didn't want anyone to feel how I was feeling day after day. As a child, I felt unloved, unwanted, I didn't fit in anywhere, never felt good enough for anybody, felt ugly, unintelligent, had a constant feeling of rejection, was bullied, abused, attacked, cheated on, a failure too. When I look at all of this, which are just some of what I've felt through my life, it's very clear to me that I have resentment stored there because it wouldn't be natural not to after having a couple of these things, let alone more. I spent my life holding back the true feelings behind Lorraine, which I know now has done me no good. However, it did help me to become a good person who has enjoyed helping others out in their time of need.

There are ways in which you can channel resentment, and hiding the truth about how you feel isn't one of them. We only punish ourselves by holding onto resentment, as it is blocking the path to us healing the hurt and pain that harbored the resentment in the first place. Feeling resentment is like being a slave to the cause of it, and in time it consumes you.

I have been doing the following throughout my life and this could be another reason why I've never thought that I resented anyone.

I've always tried to stay positive and block out those negative thoughts no matter what, because fueling negativity breeds more negativity and resentment is very happily feeding on the negativity and consuming you in the process.

I've tried my best not to bring the negative issues from past relationships into present relationships (but you can't control what your partner brings into your relationship) such as feelings of rejection, abandonment, pain and hurt. We can't control how and what others do to us but resenting them makes us their slave, so you have to find a way to let go.

In order to make peace with yourself, you have to find a way to make peace with those who have wronged you, and forgive where you can. You are showing that you're the stronger and better person.

Find something that you can do to keep your mind active on a positive note, something that you enjoy doing and can pick up when you're feeling negative and down.

*

CARRIE WORTHINGTON
Carrie was diagnosed with depression,
anxiety, and trichotillomania in 2000 at age 41

I do not feel resentment regarding my mental illness, now. I was in full denial of even having mental illness at first. I knew it was there but I did not admit it to myself, my family or even my doctors for a long time. I did feel horribly resentful when I dealt with my husband's mental illness and I felt alone. Twenty years ago, it was difficult to find someone to speak to because people just didn't understand. I was resentful sometimes when my life was swirling out of control, yet some I knew, family even, expected something different. Since my husband and I always discussed his illness, my son's, and how to handle things, we got to the point that we put our family first, and handled everyone with what our priorities and needs were first. Sometimes when I was overwhelmed with being the caregiver, and at that time the one without the illness, I did feel resentful that people didn't understand mental illness and what I was dealing with as a caregiver. This is what prompted me to become a mental illness advocate.

Right now, in my life, I have no anger or feel any resentment. This is me, who I am, illnesses and all. I do, however, get angry at people who criticize or stigmatize people with mental illness. I have jumped on many a soapbox when this arises. This is, however, something totally different than feeling resentment.

*

# CHAPTER THIRTEEN

# Dodging the Rabbit Hole

All of life is peaks and valleys. Don't let the peaks
get too high or the valleys too low. -JOHN WOODEN

Many mental illnesses can be periodic, with cycling between times of improvement and deterioration. When worsening of symptoms feels imminent, how do you manage or cope with the downward spiral?

*

ADRIANNE ALLEN-LANG
Adrianne was diagnosed with dissociative
identity disorder in 2015 at age 18

I make friends, family and loved ones aware that I think I'm going down again. They keep an eye on me in case I get really bad, and then activate my safety plan to stop the spiral. Usually I'll come out of it just fine. When I feel I'm starting to spiral, I notice patterns of negative thinking, lack of emotion, chest pain, increased widespread body pain and a decrease in sleep. I try to combat these by being mindful, and if I'm in the middle of a spiral, six out of ten times I'm now able to talk myself out of them before I need outside intervention.

\*

MORGAN BUTLER
Morgan was diagnosed with depression
and anxiety in 2009 at age 15

I am very aware of when I am being hit with a low in my depression. Sometimes I let it wash over me and I get stuck there for a little while. The best way to pull myself out of it is to verbally express my mental state, out loud. Be it to God, or a loved one, or my dog, or nobody, but I need to say it out loud to recognize what is happening and to take on my depression directly. After that, it's trying to distract myself with positive activities, or logically maneuvering my way through the maze in my head. Taking emotion out of the equation can help if there was a specific trigger. If there wasn't a trigger, sometimes I just need to listen to music or watch a certain movie, or cuddle my pet and just cry. I need to cry out loud and NOT bottle. Keeping everything pent up is what caused that turning point for me in 2009— and that's not something that I'd like to repeat.

\*

LYNDA CHELDELIN FELL
Lynda was diagnosed with depression in 2000 at age 35
and posttraumatic stress disorder in 2012 at age 47

I've become vigilant about monitoring my symptoms, because I respond much better to immediate treatment rather than waiting to see if it improves. If I ignore my symptoms, a downward spiral is in my near future. I've become as vigilant about my mental health as I have about my physical health. Self-advocacy and good care are my best preventions against falling down the rabbit hole.

\*

SHAUNA COX
Shauna was diagnosed with an
anxiety disorder in 2009 at age 26

I try to pay attention to my breathing as much as possible when I'm feeling stressed. When the anxiety starts to get worse, I find that my breathing becomes much more shallow. Sometimes I have to yawn to get a full breath in, because it's hard for me to inhale fully. I will often feel physically ill when I'm especially anxious as well, sometimes experiencing nausea and often diarrhea. I also find myself getting a bit more distracted during these times; it becomes hard to focus on anything for too long before my thoughts wander.

If finances allow, I find it helpful to see my psychologist to talk through new stressors that might be causing increased anxiety, or to work through old, resurfaced ones. Most of the time, though, I turn to loved ones. I talk to my husband, call my parents, or visit with a friend. It helps to talk to someone who understands and knows what I'm going through. Venting is therapy in itself! It helps to have someone acknowledge what I'm experiencing and help me through it.

I also try to do relaxing activities that I enjoy when the anxiety is bad. I draw a hot bath, and read in the tub. I might make popcorn and watch a movie. I'll lie on the couch with my husband with one dog curled up in between us, and the other curled up on my lap. I'll try and live as much as I can in the present, so that my thoughts center themselves there, and my worries about the past or the future fade into the background. Sometimes this is easier said than done, but it helps to at least try to go back to those favored activities. If the anxiety is nearing a ten, I will take an anxiolytic. And as always, it helps to say the mantra, "How it was in the past is not how it is now."

\*

JANE MCDONALD
Jane was diagnosed with major depressive disorder in 1989,
multiple anxiety disorders in 2001, multiple personality
disorders in 2007, and dissociative identity disorder in 2014

I often experience my mental illnesses as very cyclical. I start out feeling well, I have energy, I am social, get out of my apartment more, do things and talk to people. My mood is improved, my anxiety is significantly reduced, and my other personalities do not come out as much or are not as bothersome as they usually are. However, usually after a matter of days, sometimes a week at most, tiny things start to happen, like small cracks appearing in my life. I become more irritable, easily upset by small things. My mood won't be quite as good, and my energy levels will start to drop. I start to isolate, spend more time in my apartment and less time doing things I normally enjoy, like attending events or going to my art group. I start to avoid social contact as much as possible. I don't do my chores or take care of myself as much as I was previously. Gradually, these things become worse and worse. My mood continues to drop, my energy levels are depleted, I don't bother to take care of dishes that pile up or laundry that needs to be done. I avoid all social situations, only leaving my apartment for medical or therapy appointments. I miss out on art group, I call in sick to work, and generally isolate myself completely. The other personalities also begin to come out more often, for greater periods of time, and are more difficult to cope with.

Generally, I start to notice things going awry fairly early on, but there isn't much that I know to do to stop the downward spiral. I try to continue to do things, to maintain my mood and try to stay active. I try to make a commitment of going to work even if I don't feel like it, and going to art group, even though I may not really want to. I know that once I start isolating I will not stop for a while, so I do what I can to fight that urge. I also try to listen to upbeat music, watch funny or entertaining TV shows, and practice good self-care by showering, dressing, and doing my makeup. I try to keep up with my chores and reward myself for my efforts. Sometimes these things work, for a while. Other times they don't. Unfortunately, I have yet to figure out how to break the cycle completely and always end up in a bad place where I don't take care of myself, avoid all commitments, isolate, self-harm, and generally sleep most of the day. I try to talk to my case manager and psychiatrist to let them know when the downward spiral is starting in the hopes that they can find a way to help me at least delay this descent into darkness and chaos but, ultimately, I cannot stop it.

*

AMY OWEN
Amy was diagnosed with ADD and
bipolar disorder in 2014 at age 42

This is hard. I can sometimes feel it coming on and I talk to those around me. I try to stay away from the kids so they don't see me experience it. I sleep a lot. This helps to keep me from making things harder for me and the ones I love.

*

DENISE PURCELL
Denise was diagnosed with depression, posttraumatic stress
disorder, and dissociative identity disorder in 1995 at age 30

When I feel my depression has taken a dive, I acknowledge it and try to reason why. You can't reason with depression. There is no upside to that. I will tell my therapist, tell my psychiatrist. Since I've been on a multitude of meds, it's just more of being aware that I feel so bad. I try and think of having bad moments instead of bad days. But it's not true for me, as far as get up and start your day, fake it until you make it. No, it makes me feel worse and like I should hide how I feel. Nothing helps when I feel that bad.

*

ERICKA REEVE
Ericka was diagnosed with dissociative identity disorder, posttraumatic stress disorder, obsessive-compulsive disorder, depression, anxiety and an eating disorder in 2013 at age 26

This is right where I am in therapy. We are working through trauma and beginning to work with unknown parts and memories. It is causing more dissociative moments, depression and high stress instances. We are discussing this in therapy and the different options that may be available to me.

Without insurance, again, this makes things a bit trickier, but we work on it. I can say that now, I'm aware of when these shifts begin to happen. The fogginess and/or sinking feelings, the unworthiness many feel, and/or acting out. I recognized it and did not want to go back so far to the way things were before my diagnosis. This is why my therapist and I discussed my trying to get on medications, if I'm able to get them.

Now I try to talk to my parts openly and make them aware things will be okay. We are now safe, I am now an adult, and varying things like this. It's just a piece of the issues that can arise with DID and its many comorbidities.

*

LORRAINE SCOTT
Lorraine was diagnosed with non-epilepsy attack disorder
and dissociative identity disorder in 2016 at age 48

With my illnesses, both are unpredictable as to when they deteriorate, and it is very rare that there are any signs of improvement. It's difficult to explain how my personalities switch because sometimes I'm unaware of which one is leading and at the forefront, and I could have no memory of what's gone on in days because of this. I will however, try and explain some of what I think I know.

After having seizures or conking out, etc., of the pains that I get in my head before, during and after, will determine how severe the aftermath is. This can then last up to twenty-four hours before I'm back to functioning somewhat normal. So straight after a seizure, I will normally be confused, unaware of my surroundings and how I got there or how long I've been there, upset, feeling vulnerable, amnesia and not knowing the people around me. I can be aggressive, unaware of what I'm saying, tired and exhausted, and speaking gibberish with slurred speech.

These are just some of what I experience, which then has a major effect as to who I am when I come out of it. Normally five-year-old Lorraine will make an appearance when my vulnerability state is severe, upset. If not, it will be twelve-year-old Lorraine when feeling a higher level of vulnerability, amnesia. The other personalities that will appear will only have memories of set parts of my life but no memories on anything else that's gone on in my life. This all can be very confusing within itself, let alone trying to explain it. I think that these are all personalities that my brain created to protect me from the traumas that have happened in my life and that's where my NEAD and

DID merge into one. So sometimes I feel alert and awake, but within minutes or a couple of hours this will turn to the feeling of exhaustion, then I'll conk out and have a seizure. There isn't a day that goes by that this doesn't happen, and some days I will have clusters of back to back seizures, so since 2011, there have been no signs of improvement. As the years have gone by, we've learned more and more about what happens. For a couple of years, we kept a log of all the seizures, what happened, and when and how long from start to me being fully alert again. It was, and still is, very upsetting listening to what people would tell me had happened, as I couldn't believe that it was/is me. We also found out what some of the triggers are for me and we looked how and what we can put into place to help slow them down or even give me time where it may take longer for them to form.

The things we do include giving me a two-hour time limit to be out. After this we know a conk out and seizure is imminent. We use sunscreens on the car windows to block out bright lights, sunshine, glares, and flashing. This also prolongs the conk out for a few more minutes but when in a car for more than fifteen minutes, it's imminent that I'm going to conk out. I avoid long conversations because this wears me out and will bring on a conk out and seizure. I avoid being on the phone for more than ten minutes because I will conk out. I avoid putting extra pressure on my spine because the stress on my spine is also a trigger. Being tired and lack of sleep is a trigger. Sometimes watching TV will set them off. Noise from babies crying, kids shouting and screaming, people talking too loud, music, banging etc. will trigger them too. Any form of mental, emotional or physical stress will cause them also. If I get too excited, I will come down with a bang, literally. I'll be on the floor conked out, followed by a seizure. Overexertion and doing too much will cause physical stress on my spine. Focusing, which I have to do when in conversation, working on my laptop or computer, sewing, watching TV, wears me out very quickly. The focusing becomes straining, the straining becomes stress, and there she goes, as my family says, "She's gone." That means I've conked out. We've learned all this through years of observation and, although we can't stop them, we do our best to cope with the inevitable.

I've lived with dissociative identity disorder since the age of five, although I've only learned of this twelve months ago. I've lived my life unaware of any changes in me, and I'm still learning about this illness. My family says they've always known I've got split personalities, but never made an issue of it. They say "That's Lorraine," nothing more or nothing less. Most people would have just called me a naughty girl, easily distracted, and a day dreamer. I was very impatient with little to no tolerance level. They didn't know it was something more. I'm not fully aware of the triggers that make me switch, but I do think there is a link with NEAD and DID because only certain identities show after the seizures. The other identities are triggered when traumatic things happen or I need protecting. If I've been mentally hurt, then protective Lorraine will come to the forefront and stick around until she feels the source has gone, and then she'll settle back down again. I can have up to eight or more different identities who will surface depending on the situation. I'm still in the process of identifying them, but this could take years, as some may not appear for years. Unfortunately, I don't know a lot about these because I'm quite new to this, and also I blackout so I don't know what each has said or done.

It's very difficult because I know in the past I've argued with a previous boyfriend and ended the relationship, and after a few days when placid Lorraine is back, she's wondering "why isn't he talking to me or contacted me, what have I done to upset him?" I've asked myself and then when I've been told of what went down I've been so upset because I've had no memory of it. I couldn't tell him that because I know he would have ended the relationship anyway, thinking she's crazy. I've had to apologize time after time and just fob it off with "I was having a bad day," and each time I promised that it wouldn't happen again but, yes it did numerous times until one day he couldn't take it anymore. During all of this, I remember telling him to ignore if I say that I want us to break up, but I really didn't have any idea as to what was going on with me. It's like one of the Lorraines was happy in love with him and the others didn't like him because he was somehow mentally torturing her. So when they surfaced, they would end the relationship to protect the real soft, gentle Lorraine. This went on for five years with him, so I can understand that he had enough.

Another situation was that my kids would tell me that I said things and I would have no memory of it and swear black is white because I really had no clue of anything they would be talking about. Some of the stuff would have been months prior to me being told, and that showed that some of my switches were for months or even years. There is so much I have lost in my life, whichever Lorraine is at the forefront, they have all missed a lot. There's not much at the moment that I know I can do to prevent this from happening. It's very upsetting and scary and I hate it when I wake up and I don't know where the past few hours, or days, or months, or years have gone. I can't imagine what my kids must have been thinking of me when they were growing up. But what I do know is they love their mother no matter what, and they know that it doesn't matter which one is me, I will be the backbone of the family and protect them, whatever the cost. They are my life and my all. The only thing they can do is to go with whichever Lorraine is there and avoid upsetting them.

I will avoid situations where any aggression is around and if someone's going to fight, I will try and defuse it. I fear one Lorraine, and that's the fighter. She hasn't been out since I was thirteen, in secondary school. I knew about her but not the DID, so I would say that was my bad side, which I have kept locked away since.

Unfortunately, it's not always easy to avoid situations because you can't control what others do, what their reactions are going to be or their response. For me, it was best to avoid aggressive, intimidating, confrontational and physically aggressive situations at all times when possible. I'm quite good at sensing when someone or something is going to kick off, so I will disappear to avoid a switch, especially if it can't be defused. These are the strategies that I have in place that hopefully avoid triggers, but as we all know in life, you never know how a situation is going to escalate or pan out, but having some baselines in place is helpful.

*

CARRIE WORTHINGTON
Carrie was diagnosed with depression,
anxiety, and trichotillomania in 2000 at age 41

The only time when I was not aware of any strange behavior was when I was experiencing my Paxil withdrawal. I knew something was wrong. Afterwards, when I was better, I was told that I did things that I was not even aware of. Work people told me that when I came back to work, I was slurring my words. My daughter told me I was mean at times. I was never aware of any of that. I feel that I was in total psychosis for about four weeks, that I was really unaware of any reality. Eventually, my mind was returning to normal. I am very blessed and grateful that going through that was temporary. I only have one or two symptoms left after five years, but my mind, actions and memory are normal. Sometimes, I feel overwhelmed with learning to live alone, the depression kicks in and I either push myself to do what I need to do, or sometimes I arrange a day when I make sure I have no responsibilities that day and actually give myself a do-nothing day. I don't lay in bed, but I catch up on the computer, watch a movie, do some things around the house and just "be." With my anxiety, I have tried to not project or ruminate the thoughts that start and bring me up to anxiety. If I'm feeling very anxious, I try to meditate, practice my breathing, or start just turning the thoughts around. I have been successful these days much more of the time.

This has been through years of therapy, reading self-help books, learning to meditate, exercising, and a determination that I never imagined I had. I have learned to not have the major pity parties I once threw myself. Once in a while it will start to creep in, but more often than not, I am aware of the thoughts that are starting to form and will figure out ways to change that direction.

*

# CHAPTER FOURTEEN

# working with Health Insurance

Today we have a health insurance industry where the first and foremost goal is to maximize profits for shareholders and CEOs, not to cover patients who have fallen ill or to compensate doctors and hospitals for their services. DIANNE FEINSTEIN

In years past, many health insurance companies provided better coverage for physical illness than they did for mental illness. A law passed in 2008, the Paul Wellstone and Pete Domenici Mental Health Parity and Addiction Equity Act, now requires coverage of mental and behavioral health services to be comparable to physical health coverage. What has been your experience with health insurance covering treatments related to your mental illness?

\*

ADRIANNE ALLEN-LANG
Adrianne was diagnosed with dissociative
identity disorder in 2015 at age 18

I live in Australia, so Medicare covers the bulk of my medical expenses.

\*

LYNDA CHELDELIN FELL
Lynda was diagnosed with depression in 2000 at age 35
and posttraumatic stress disorder in 2012 at age 47

Our health insurance covers medication and medical care, but counseling coverage is limited. We're covered by two insurances, and we still have to pay out of pocket for psychologist appointments.

\*

SHAUNA COX
Shauna was diagnosed with an
anxiety disorder in 2009 at age 26

I am fortunate that I live in Canada where healthcare doesn't cost anything (aside from paying taxes). However, while seeing a psychiatrist or a family doctor is free, visits with a psychologist are not. The wait time to see a psychiatrist is fairly long in my province, and I wouldn't be able to get in weekly. As such, the talking portion of therapy wouldn't be hugely beneficial. I can get into my family doctor quickly but he is limited to dispensing medication when it comes to therapy and can't really talk me through issues. Ideally, I would be able to go to a psychologist weekly, or at least monthly, for therapy. Unfortunately, visits with a psychologist tend to be expensive.

I have had coverage under work benefits to see a psychologist, but this tends to only cover one or two visits a year, at the most. My husband and I make too much money to qualify for any additional assistance to help pay for a psychologist, but not enough money that we can afford me going every month for treatment.

While I know that, compared to other countries, Canada is very generous to its population when it comes to healthcare, I wish that mental illness was considered along the same lines as physical illness.

Mental illness can cause the same amount, or an even greater amount, of suffering in people as physical illness and needs to be treated just as seriously.

*

JANE MCDONALD
Jane was diagnosed with major depressive disorder in 1989,
multiple anxiety disorders in 2001, multiple personality
disorders in 2007, and dissociative identity disorder in 2014

Where I live in Ontario, Canada, our health insurance is different from in the United States. We have a public healthcare system. This is not to say this is ideal, however. Psychotherapy from a psychologist, for instance, is not covered under our public healthcare system and therefore must be paid for out of pocket or by private insurance, which many can't afford. At one hundred and fifty dollars or more an hour, this is simply not an option.

Psychiatrists are covered but finding one who is taking on new patients is a nightmare, as the majority are already overworked and have huge caseloads. Once you find a psychiatrist, many of them do not provide any form of therapy, and only do medication consultations. Even getting in just to discuss medications often occur only once every three or four weeks, leaving people to struggle with side effects or ineffective medications for much longer than necessary.

General physicians prefer not to handle psychiatric medications because they are not specialized in it. My own psychiatrist, when I first moved to my current city, only did medications and I was able to see him only once every month or two. He overmedicated me severely. At one point I was taking seven different medications five times a day. It wasn't feasible and I ended up struggling a great deal. If I complained about how hard it was, my concerns fell on deaf ears.

Fortunately, I now have an excellent psychiatrist who not only handles medications but also provides psychotherapy. I am able to see him once every two to three weeks for thirty to forty-five minutes at a time. I am extremely grateful to have him and it took me ten years to find him after moving to my city. I was only able to find him as a referral through another program in the community that I was attending. I was finishing this program and had no outside community support other than my over-medicating psychiatrist and inept family physician. I had no case manager, social worker, psychologist, or anyone else so the leader of the program I was in, made some phone calls after she saw that I myself had attempted to contact no fewer than six psychiatrists, and had no luck with any of them. Fortunately, there was a psychiatrist who was affiliated with the same large organization that had run the program I was in and so he was willing, with some persuasion and begging on my part, to take me on. I have been with him for two years at this point and am very grateful.

Accessing mental healthcare, particularly at the professional level, is a real struggle where I live. There are community agencies that offer limited counseling, but often you can only attend for six sessions. Anyone requiring more in-depth, long-term therapy is stuck waiting years for a psychiatrist—if they are lucky enough to even find one. Hospitals deal with individuals in crisis but there is very little follow up or help once the patient is released, and fewer beds are available for inpatient wards.

Other community mental health agencies offer services such as case management, which I am now a client of, but these individuals are often not as professionally trained. They can provide general assistance, but not any kind of actual treatment. They assist more with day-to-day tasks of self-care, employment, volunteering, housing, accessing general healthcare and other community-based resources.

The agency I am with has a psychiatrist on staff, but it takes months to get in to see him for a ten-minute appointment and even then he simply prescribes medications. I am fortunate enough to not have to rely on his services, as I have a psychiatrist of my own. Even within this agency, there is a two-year limitation of services so if you require more long-term or in-depth care, you are once more left out in the cold.

Simply put, there is not enough professional, long-term, in-depth counseling available for those with severe mental illness. As a result, many people fall through the cracks and end up in emergency waiting rooms but are often turned away even from there, as there are not enough beds in the psychiatric wings. There are a few private hospitals but most beds will cost out-of-pocket. The few beds covered by public healthcare require at least a year's waiting.

Although people rave about having public healthcare here in Canada, the fact of the matter is that it is simply not adequate. If you need anything in-depth such as psychological or psychiatric counseling, you are left waiting years for services and often have to pay yourself. Many of us with mental illness simply cannot afford to wait years and years for help.

*

AMY OWEN
Amy was diagnosed with ADD and
bipolar disorder in 2014 at age 42

I am lucky to have good insurance but the cost is overwhelming. I worry about paying for it.

\*

DENISE PURCELL
Denise was diagnosed with depression, posttraumatic stress
disorder, and dissociative identity disorder in 1995 at age 30

This is a problem for mental illness patients. If you are lucky to have insurance coverage that might include mental health, they limit visits. If you are in the middle of receiving help and then have to stop your treatment when you are not finished, it's detrimental. If you don't have personal insurance coverage then you are part of the system which consists of clinics. Most therapists are limited to social work, addictions, etc. They don't have specialty psychiatrists available for more complex mental illnesses. That leaves us alone, and frustrated and stuck in a system known by a number, not a name. If you do get a psychiatrist or med person it's a limit of fifteen minutes in and out. That's barely enough time to say anything.

\*

ERICKA REEVE
Ericka was diagnosed with dissociative identity disorder,
posttraumatic stress disorder, obsessive-compulsive disorder,
depression, anxiety and an eating disorder in 2013 at age 26

Ha, ha! Health insurance. I haven't had it in so long, it's now a distant memory. It is indeed unaffordable for those who have multiple conditions the way I do, and inadequate. Every single area within health coverage needs improvement. Treatment is unattainable for many, as they aren't us, and don't have parts like I do. I cannot fathom what it must be like, so in that way I find myself fortunate to have DID. They help tremendously. I thought I was alone most of my life, but actually being alone and trying to figure out how to get the help many people require, I can't imagine.

*

LORRAINE SCOTT
Lorraine was diagnosed with non-epilepsy attack disorder
and dissociative identity disorder in 2016 at age 48

Living in the UK, tax payers (those who work and pay tax or have worked and paid tax) contribute toward NHS costs each month, so then any medical treatment we need we get without having to complete forms or pay any extra costs. The government also plows funds in, as there are people who don't work. You can, however, have private treatment and pay for that out of your own pocket. This is the better of the two but it is very costly so people on low wages may not be able to afford these costs. The NHS is good, but unfortunately you are put on waiting lists for any treatment that you need and this can be a lengthy process. It doesn't always prove to give you the best of treatments and a lot of people have different thoughts as to how good or bad it is. Luckily those who can afford it have the choice to go private, whereas those on low incomes do not have that luxury.

*

CARRIE WORTHINGTON
Carrie was diagnosed with depression,
anxiety, and trichotillomania in 2000 at age 41

When my husband was being treated for his bipolar over twenty-five years ago, it was horrible, the health coverage was very stigmatized and there was not parity between mental and physical health. Up to about six years ago, only twenty-seven states had a law restricting parity between the mental health and physical health coverage. In the last ten years, the coverage improved, having to pay the specialist co-pay, but at least there was some coverage. The cost of the medication was much higher because a lot of it fell under the specialty drug coverage. Now, after the Affordable Care Act, it is against the law to distinguish between mental health treatment and physical health treatment. My therapist appointment is under doctor visits on the insurance lists, no longer stigmatizing my treatment. Same with the hospital coverage. I believe there has to be better coverage, more affordable treatment, even free, in order to avoid many complications later in life. If you can treat a child that is part of a domestic violence home, give them treatment to handle/deal with/understand what is going on when they are school age, the complications for later life hardship can be avoided. If you start treatment and therapy with a child that is starting to show signs of a mental illness, the chances of them being a very successful, stable adult are very good. Classes, seminars, and groups like what NAMI offers are essential in the understanding, treatment and bringing it to the forefront of illnesses that can be managed.

It has been a travesty that when states have to cut budgets, the first to go are social services, which includes low-cost or free health coverage. Most of our state hospitals are closed and the local hospitals are expected to get subsidized for any kind of treatment. But most clinics and hospitals are ill equipped to handle the true needs that are out there today. People fall through the cracks and live a life that doesn't have to be so difficult, therapy and meds could assist in being stable and a self-sufficient person (okay, stepping off the soapbox now).

*

# CHAPTER FIFTEEN

# Facing Our Fears

The oldest and strongest emotion of mankind is fear, and the oldest and strongest kind of fear is fear of the unknown. -H. P. LOVECRAFT

Mental illness is a riddle wrapped in a mystery inside an enigma. It is somewhat of an orphan illness that falls across several different medical specialties resulting in confusion, myths, and taboos. At the root of it all are millions who juggle stigma, misdiagnoses, and lack of health insurance. What do you fear most about having mental illness?

*

ADRIANNE ALLEN-LANG
Adrianne was diagnosed with dissociative
identity disorder in 2015 at age 18

What I fear most is ending up alone. I fear not being able to ever function well enough to form a secure attachment with someone other than my own child, and not being able to function as a cognitive member of society. My illness stems from trauma and isolation, and that's the last thing I want to experience for the rest of my days. I fear

I'm going to be alone and that I'm going to ruin my son's childhood. I know they're both irrational fears as everyone can be loved and I'm a great mother, but that doesn't stop that demon in the back of your head, putting you down.

*

MORGAN BUTLER
Morgan was diagnosed with depression
and anxiety in 2009 at age 15

I have a few main fears about having depression and anxiety:

- Employers not understanding or undervaluing me due to my mental illness

- My mental illness getting in the way of settling down in a permanent romantic relationship

- Risk of postpartum depression if I have kids

I'm sure there are more, but those are the three that are most on my mind now. I used to fear being able to withstand my depression to live past the age of twenty. But here I am, twenty-four, and still kicking. I've learned how to be meticulous in exposing my mental illness to others, but I have become much more open about it in recent years. Since it is so stigmatized, I feel that I need to be open about it for my own health and for others. I don't want someone to treat me any differently or worse than others because of my depression and anxiety. I just hope for compassion, as I'd like to offer to others, too.

\*

LYNDA CHELDELIN FELL
Lynda was diagnosed with depression in 2000 at age 35
and posttraumatic stress disorder in 2012 at age 47

Having lost a child, I don't fear much as I've already faced the worst. But in relation to depression and PTSD, I fear that one day my body won't respond to medication and I'll end up bedridden like my great-grandmother. Logically, I believe that won't happen, but it's a fear nonetheless. I also fear that our work to de-stigmatize mental illness won't be enough, and my grandchildren will inherit the same problems we face today. That would be a tragedy, to my mind.

Finally, I fear that by being so open about my own mental illness, someone will discredit all my advocacy work and professional endeavors. I fear someone judging me to be unstable because I carry the diagnoses of depression and posttraumatic stress disorder. I was born a highly sensitive individual, and the thought of critics casting shadows of doubt over my work because of mental illness is a very real fear. But if we aren't brave in this generation, the next will inherit the same problem. And so I am determined to stand alongside others who use their own experiences to pave the fields and plant seeds of hope for this generation, and the next.

\*

SHAUNA COX
Shauna was diagnosed with an
anxiety disorder in 2009 at age 26

There are several things that I've feared about having a mental illness, but these qualms have changed, and in some cases have also lessened over time. My husband and I don't have kids yet, but I used to fret that my disorder would negatively impact our children if we did become parents. When the anxiety was a ten, and it was hard for me to go anywhere without my husband, I would think about how that could affect our potential children. Would I be able to go to the park with our kids on my own or would I have a panic attack while there? Could I bring them swimming by myself or would I have an attack and need to rush them out of the pool? I worried that they would see me have an anxiety attack, and develop the same problem as a result.

Now that the anxiety has improved, I don't have the same misgivings anymore. I do still fear, however, my kids having an anxiety disorder if there is a genetic component to the illness. No one wants their kids to suffer or to go through hardship. It pains me to think that I might have a disorder that our children could inherit. I know that there is nothing I can do to change my genes, and so I have had to learn to let this uneasiness go as it is out of my control.

One fear I have that hasn't changed with time is that the anxiety disorder could potentially hold me back in life. When I have had to change jobs in the past, the anxiety has been at the top of my mind. I think about whether I could "handle" the job with my disorder, and about how understanding a potential boss might be. While I am lucky that I am at a job that I love, I do sometimes wonder what I would do if I ever had to leave the vet clinic that I work at. I worry that the anxiety would near a ten again, and that I would be right back to where I started.

I know that the disorder has already held me back in some ways. My husband and I have been on a couple cruises. The cruise ships often offer various tours at the different ports of call. There have been trips that I have been interested in, but then the old fear returns of needing a bathroom close by in case an anxiety attack washes over me, and I pick a safer option instead of one that might be more fun. While this has also improved with time, I do fear that I will never progress to the point where the anxiety I go through isn't a consideration anymore.

Eventually (probably not until we retire), my husband and I would like to move to Newfoundland to be closer to family. It troubles me that the anxiety may hold us back from that dream as well, or that it will get bad again if and when we do move. While I know that I had problems with anxiety when I lived in Ontario, it didn't progress to the point where I needed medication or therapy until we moved to Alberta. I wonder sometimes if that was a trigger to the disorder progressing, and whether another move would increase the anxiety all over again.

*

JANE MCDONALD
Jane was diagnosed with major depressive disorder in 1989,
multiple anxiety disorders in 2001, multiple personality
disorders in 2007, and dissociative identity disorder in 2014

It is difficult to say what I fear most, as my fears tend to change over the course of weeks, months or years. Sometimes they even change daily. On good days, for example, I fear that my energy, my better mood, or my reduced anxiety won't last. I fear that the demons of depression and dissociation will take over once more, plummeting me into a pit of darkness that swallows me whole for weeks or even months. I fear the loss of functioning that happens with this.

I fear losing time at work, losing relationships as I withdraw and isolate, and I fear losing support of friends and family. Sometimes I fear the uncertainty that comes with living with other personalities. I have little to no control over who comes out, and what they will say and do. I have lack of awareness about what happens from a few minutes to several hours, or even for a whole day or two.

I fear that my self-destructive alter will harm me (us?) and do serious damage. I fear she will try to electrocute us again or that she will cut me badly enough that I pass out from blood loss (or worse).

I fear that my youngest alters will come out in public, particularly the one who is always scared and does not (cannot?) speak. I fear that they will get upset and that I will not be aware enough to comfort them, to get them to a safe space, to protect them.

I have woken up having been cut, having had my youngest one out, scared and unable to ask for help. I have woken up standing in the middle of a road with cars honking at me to get out of the way. I worry that my angry alter will say or do hurtful things to friends, family, or even my case manager, doctor, psychiatrist, or other supporters, and they'll decide it isn't worth helping me, and will give up on me.

On the darkest days, I fear that I will never get completely better, or that on one of my worst days my mental illness will result in my death. I fear that the depression will never let up, that the anxiety will never be manageable, and that I will get to the point where I am just not able to fight anymore. I fear that I will take my own life during one of these dark episodes and, in doing so, will hurt my friends and family. I fear that there will come a time when there is simply no light at the end of the tunnel.

\*

AMY OWEN
Amy was diagnosed with ADD and
bipolar disorder in 2014 at age 42

I fear for my kids. I don't want them to go through what I have. I fear being judged my whole life. I fear messing up more than I already have and not being able to fix those mistakes. The longer I live with the disorder, the more fears I have. I feel that is because I want to be normal and not have all these problems. I worry about staying on my meds, I take them religiously but life can change. That scares me.


\*

DENISE PURCELL
Denise was diagnosed with depression, posttraumatic stress
disorder, and dissociative identity disorder in 1995 at age 30

That people believe I'm not a stable or capable person. That I won't be taken seriously or that my thoughts or ideas are because I have a mental illness, instead of my own ideas. Just because someone might have a mental illness, doesn't mean everything or anything they say or believe is nonsense. If anything we have a better insight about things and can be very caring and compassionate people.


\*

ERICKA REEVE
Ericka was diagnosed with dissociative identity disorder,
posttraumatic stress disorder, obsessive-compulsive disorder,
depression, anxiety and an eating disorder in 2013 at age 26

Fears? None really. I was confused before. I have concerns in a way, but I do not think or feel the way a typical person does. One thing that has come up for us is that the more we speak, the more it has the potential to negatively affect my siblings, friends who support us, and my husband. These people can be ferociously protective of myself and my parts, so we do not want the things people will inevitably say to them about me to bring them down.

For my parts, there are many fears, but one of the most prominent is stigma. The stigma surrounding all mental illness is morally repugnant, grotesque, and to put it simply, wrong. It's wrong. My parts work tirelessly to combat and end this, spreading awareness every way they can and to anyone that will listen. One of my protectors, a few probably, fear that more children will become the adult who I was. They speak to doctors more and more in the hopes this won't occur.

\*

LORRAINE SCOTT
Lorraine was diagnosed with non-epilepsy attack disorder
and dissociative identity disorder in 2016 at age 48

Having mental illnesses can be very lonely because you don't truly know how others will accept you now that you are linked with a mental illness. Although it shouldn't matter what illness you have, as long as it gets sorted out and you get better, there are some disorders that carry a lot of stigma, including mental illness. This is my biggest fear, and I worry how people will perceive me once they learn I have mental illnesses. I shouldn't have to worry about it, but unfortunately it is one of the biggest issues out there. The reason why we feel this way is because we need support from those around us, we want to be able to carry on the feeling that we are accepted within society and the work place. We just want to still be socially accepted, supported and understood, but this doesn't always happen when the words "mental illness" are dropped.

I'm going to list all my fears about having mental illnesses, most of which have already happened to me.

- Secrecy: I have kept the fact that my illnesses come under mental illnesses away from the majority of people because of how they will react not in front of my face, but behind my back. The gossiping and raised eyebrows, the laughing and being the talk of the town for the next week or so. I've always felt unaccepted and that's stemmed from the feeling of being an unwanted child and growing up thinking that. So, because of this, I've always had to try harder to fit in. It's been difficult not knowing if someone genuinely likes you or they are just being nice to your face. As I've gotten older, I don't do this. I'm just naturally me, if you don't like me then that's your choice.

- Discrimination: Although I no longer work, I fear having to go back to work and having to complete an application form and having to divulge that I had a mental illness. That would upset me, knowing that I would then be fully judged on that rather than my abilities to do the job. This is so unfair and it does happen.

- Isolation: This I do feel, because even though it's always been a fear, it is happening for me right now and has been for the past six years. I was a people person who would be out and about all the time, working hard, having fun with my kids and family and friends, and loved socializing. This isn't the same now. I still have fun with my kids but the rest is no more. A lot of it is because of the symptoms of my illnesses and NEAD is very unpredictable as to when the seizures are going to happen, but sometimes there are warning signs. Either way, it restricts me in what I can do. However, I do have a safe network of my kids, close friends and some family who do their utmost to help me achieve getting out and about and having some form of fun. We all need this.

- Stereotyping: This is a classic, and one that we all may feel a fear of. Unfortunately, we can't educate those who don't want to be educated, but are very quick to judge those with mental illnesses; stereotyping them is the easiest thing for them to do. I know that I am normal, the same as you all and whatever traumas I/we have experienced in life, is the root of it all.

- Embarrassment and shame: Because of stigma and stereotyping of those who have mental illnesses, it is unfair that we are made to feel this way by others. I felt embarrassed at first, but now I don't care what people think. Those who are important to me, and me being important to them, are there for me on a daily basis and don't see my illnesses as a hindrance to them. They aren't ashamed of being around me because of what others may think of people with mental illness. Society is so cruel at times and people do disengage from you.

- Black sheep of the family: This title I did have, because I was different. With having seizures and clearly switching personalities from such a young age, it seemed like I was a burden and problem child. I know my mother had her hands full, so I don't judge her for that. She did her best and had a lot to cope with, and then my behavior issues and seizures on top of all of the other stuff. She had a very traumatic life herself, and at times she couldn't cope with it all, but she was expected to or she would be classed as a weak, unfit person.

- Relationships: This is another big fear of mine because it was proven to me straight away that because I've been diagnosed with having a mental illness, that one didn't want to be associated with me or have to deal with it and give me the support that I need. This has been the biggest struggle, feeling like I have a disease that is contagious and ugly, along with no longer being good enough or acceptable. The problem is it doesn't just end there with what my husband did. I now feel that if ever I tell another man, he too will swiftly run away. This has totally dissolved any or what little confidence that I had, and I haven't any self-esteem either now. I feel ashamed, stereotyped, socially excluded and embarrassed. These are all the feelings that have reared just from this one person's actions. Now I can't help but fear that this will repeat itself time and time again from any man who shows me any interest. I'll be wondering whether he will do the same once he learns I have a mental illness. This has put me in a negative mode when it comes to thinking of relationships. It doesn't matter how much people say you're beautiful inside and out, and you deserve better than him. I will only fear the same thing happening over and over again. It's such a shame that people don't think about the effects their tongue may have, and the destructive damage it can have. So, the fear of not being wanted and living a lonely life is very strong for me and scares me so much that I won't even explore the options. I couldn't cope with rejection again.

- Getting better: I do fear that my illnesses will deteriorate and get worse. I know my spinal problem is deteriorating and I fear this will be the same with my mental illnesses and that they will develop into something else in years to come.

Even though I have these fears, with some of them I am learning to not worry or let them over cloud my mind in getting the help that I need to get better. You can't control how others are going to react to you, and in saying that, it does make me switch off from those who I see have no interest in learning more information about what you're going through and why. I just see that some people are shallow and uneducated on mental illness. But that's just some who I've come across, it doesn't speak for all. But if you know someone has an illness, it's best to educate yourself about that illness so you can have some understanding as to what and how they feel, and also what you can do to help them. That's what I would do, anyway.

*

CARRIE WORTHINGTON
Carrie was diagnosed with depression,
anxiety, and trichotillomania in 2000 at age 41

I don't have many fears about having mental illness. My anxiety and depression, as I've learned, can be managed. I'm also getting better about dealing with any symptoms that come up. This is a new concept, as I have resisted meds for many years. Then I felt I would never come out of the depression and anxiety caused by my grief for my husband. I felt like I would never crawl out of the deep pit I felt I was in. Every day I had to live without him caused me anxiety. Now, I know I can change thoughts, actions and the direction of the way my mind thinks. It is not easy, I'm not always successful but I have come very far in the last few years. There has not been one thought of hopelessness in the last two years. I do have fear and loneliness, but not despair. I look forward to having a very manageable mental health life. My goal would be, of course, to reduce the meds, but they help me. So if I have to take some type of meds for the rest of my life, so be it. It is working.

CHAPTER SIXTEEN

# Identifying Our Obstacles

Life is made up, not of great sacrifices or duties, but of little things, in which smiles and kindness, and small obligations given habitually, are what preserve the heart and secure comfort. -HUMPHRY DAVY

Mental illness sometimes feels as if we have embarked on a foreign journey with no companion, compass, or light. Along the way, we encounter many obstacles including societal judgment, health insurance, and shadows of self-doubt. What do you find are the hardest obstacles about living with a mental illness?

\*

ADRIANNE ALLEN-LANG
Adrianne was diagnosed with dissociative
identity disorder in 2015 at age 18

Definitely the stigma attached with mental illness is a huge obstacle. Every job I apply for, every doctor I go to, every time I get my medication refilled. It's horrid. People need to understand that we are just people too, and we're just sick. You don't shame someone for a broken arm or leg, so why do we do it for a broken mind? The hardest obstacles for me are the little things. Making phone calls, getting out of bed, eating, showering. I want people to know that we aren't doing it due to being lazy or unmotivated. Mental illness is actually that, an illness of the brain. We wouldn't shame someone with cancer for having trouble looking after themselves, so why do we with mental health?

\*

LYNDA CHELDELIN FELL
Lynda was diagnosed with depression in 2000 at age 35
and posttraumatic stress disorder in 2012 at age 47

I think my biggest obstacle is the stigma. We immediately envision a homeless person rambling on the sidewalk. We use derogatory terms such as "gone postal" to reference a person who has snapped, lost their mind, become mentally unstable. When a physical illness is left untreated, our body becomes unstable. If a mental illness is left untreated, yes, our mind becomes unstable, but that doesn't mean we're a threat to the public. Not every terrorist is mentally unstable. And not every person living with mental illness is a threat. The sooner we break the stigma about mental illness, the better off we'll be as a society.

\*

SHAUNA COX
Shauna was diagnosed with an
anxiety disorder in 2009 at age 26

One of the hardest obstacles to living with a mental illness is finding it harder to do things that other people take for granted. I wish that I never had to give a second thought to going shopping, or traveling, or changing jobs. These are things that most people can do either without or with a much smaller amount of anxiety than I can. Everything that I do in life seems to come with a, "Can I handle this without having an anxiety attack?" thought.

Anything new in my life is often approached with anxiety in the forefront of my mind. No matter how far I've progressed since first being diagnosed with an anxiety disorder, there can be new experiences that bring me right back to where I started. I recently received a letter in the mail summoning me for jury duty. This is a huge responsibility in Canada, and one that I don't take lightly. I want to serve as best as I can. It's also exciting, as the legal process is something that intrigues me. However, one of the first thoughts that went through my mind upon opening the summons was, what if I'm sitting in the courtroom and an anxiety attack hits? A courtroom is a place where it might be impossible or embarrassing to have to make a quick exit in the event of an attack. I don't know if I can do this!

Mental illness is a reason for being excused from serving on a jury, and I thought about using the anxiety disorder as a reason for why I can't serve. I have a couple days before I have to mail in my response, and I'm still on the fence as to whether I think I can handle the experience. If I do go, I will likely need an antianxiety medication to get through it, but then how good of a juror would I be?

Another obstacle that I think is somewhat unique to those living with mental illnesses is that talking about having a mental illness is still considered taboo. People are often surprised by my willingness to talk about what I've gone through, and what I continue to go through on an almost daily basis. A lot of people going through similar problems are too embarrassed to share with others because they fear possible reactions. Many mental illnesses are still misunderstood in today's society. One might worry that people will respond with fear or criticism to an admission of a mental illness, or that one might be judged negatively for it, without any justifiable reason. I think the best way to tackle this obstacle is to talk about mental illness whenever possible. It's important to be open and honest to the greatest extent that one feels comfortable so that the barriers and taboos get broken down. People need to be accepted and supported for their mental illness just as someone with a physical illness would be.

*

JANE MCDONALD
Jane was diagnosed with major depressive disorder in 1989,
multiple anxiety disorders in 2001, multiple personality
disorders in 2007, and dissociative identity disorder in 2014

The things I find hardest about my mental illness, change on almost a daily basis. While some mental illnesses may be in remission or stabilized, such as my depression or anxiety, other aspects can be flaring up, such as my personality disorders or my dissociation. I think one of the things I find most difficult about this is the unpredictability and ever changing nature of my mental health. One day I can be fine in some respects, but not functioning well in others. Other days I can be functioning in the aspects that I was unable to handle a few days earlier, and doing well in the things I was struggling with before.

Right now, I find many of the tasks of daily living difficult. I find it difficult to shower, dress, brush my hair and teeth, even to get out of bed at times. I find it difficult to focus on things like writing, doing dishes, washing clothes, or even watching a movie or TV show. I am also finding it difficult to go to work or attend events or places in the community. I find it difficult to cook, menu plan, grocery shop, or even just to force myself to eat at times.

Another challenge is facing the stigma and misunderstandings that are still so prevalent in society. Although things have improved in this respect, I have had friends and family who still judge me, tell me I'm faking it or doing it for the attention, and express other harsh feelings toward me. As a result, I feel I have to keep certain mental illnesses, particularly my personality disorders and dissociative identity disorder, a secret from even the closest friends. As you might imagine, this is difficult to do. How do you deal with family when your two-year-old nonverbal alter comes out and is petrified of something but can't express what?

The fear of someone finding out the truth and judging, hurting, or otherwise abandoning me can be a real challenge. I recently elected to tell a woman who I thought was a close friend about my dissociative identity disorder. She told me that I was faking it, and doing it for attention. I had a case manager tell me that DID didn't actually exist, and that I didn't have multiple personalities. To be invalidated in this way by close friends and even by mental health professionals can be devastating. It causes me to second-guess myself, and to feel ashamed. It makes it difficult to trust anyone and to open up about my challenges.

*

AMY OWEN
Amy was diagnosed with ADD and
bipolar disorder in 2014 at age 42

Getting things done in the best, most productive way. Being the best mom I can be. Doing my job to the best of my abilities. Just being the best person I can.

\*

DENISE PURCELL
Denise was diagnosed with depression, posttraumatic stress
disorder, and dissociative identity disorder in 1995 at age 30

I may be more reclusive, but I'm not stuck up. It's a defense, not a personal attack on anyone. I deserve respect and to be my own advocate for what I need. To be taken seriously when I talk. How else will you know how to help me? Don't stick me with a label. I'm a person, unique, not a text book definition. I can't do everything that some people can. I may have limits to social activities, triggers and need medication. Don't judge me. You don't know what I've been through and I would give you the same respect. Mental illness doesn't mean crazy or violent. It means that something happened and you developed a mental illness. Not everyone in mental health are criminals or untrustworthy.


\*

ERICKA REEVE
Ericka was diagnosed with dissociative identity disorder,
posttraumatic stress disorder, obsessive-compulsive disorder,
depression, anxiety and an eating disorder in 2013 at age 26

Before my diagnoses, the issues were clear and yet not at all. I was blacking out and ending up places I had no recollection of. I could not function. My parts worked various jobs when they could, but being around people was always difficult. We worked with children, and we were very good at it. Now though, our obstacles are a bit different. For me, I know what is going on in my life most days, but that doesn't mean certain things still aren't triggered and we struggle. Sleep is the hardest aspect about living with mental illness for me. I will go a week at times without it and that becomes a massive difficulty. We work together on this, but it becomes painful and I become physically ill. On numerous occasions I felt awful and ended up in the hospital, but had no real idea that it was my lack of sleep that was causing the problem, as I was unaware I had gone without sleep for so long. When I made an attempt to rest, one of my parts would take over, stay up and go. This has gotten better over the years, though sleep is still a massive hurdle for us.

*

LORRAINE SCOTT
Lorraine was diagnosed with non-epilepsy attack disorder
and dissociative identity disorder in 2016 at age 48

The main obstacle is the system improvements that are needed when it comes to mental health treatments and support. Here in the UK, we need more professionals in the mental health sector because more and more people on a daily basis are being diagnosed with a mental illness disorder, and the numbers are rapidly increasing. The system is failing its users and this is so unfair to us all, our families and friends, and the users. The amount of pressure that is put on those who are not professional mental health therapists or psychiatrists is unreal. They wouldn't let just anyone go into surgery and perform an operation, yet they are expecting untrained, uneducated people or people with no insight on your feelings to support you, the person in need of treatment. It could be that you are in need of severe treatment, but often enough you get lost in the system of waiting for years for treatment, which by then could be too late. A lot of people don't know how to give this kind of support, and also may not know what to say. They could even say the wrong thing which only makes you feel worse, or even trigger symptoms. This pressure shouldn't be put on untrained people.

The support we should be getting from family and friends includes helping us get out of bed in the morning, reminding us how important it is to eat and drink, and reassuring us that they are there to support us, no matter what. Also, helping us to organize a safe plan, offering to take us out even if it's just for a coffee and a chat, and giving us support with day-to-day living are really helpful.

The government really needs to make more resources available and lower the waiting times, as this is so unfair to all. I do however think that since being a child, the system has gotten worse and the waiting times have definitely gotten worse, the suicide rates have gone up tremendously too, but there doesn't seem to be the help out there that's needed by the users. If you go to your doctors, they will offer you medication to suppress your thoughts. How is this helping you to face and deal with the problem? I'm not saying that I'm against suppressants, but I feel it's better to deal with the root cause and build on getting you better, but suppressing is only prolonging the torture.

The next obstacle is the stigma around mental illnesses. How people see someone with a mental illness. They hear the word and judge, whether it's kept in their own mind or out loud. They don't look at the effects it has on the sufferer, good or bad, on a daily basis. One day you could be smiling, and yet the next day struggling to smile at anything. Now it doesn't mean you have to have a reason why you're struggling to smile, you just are. Some people expect there to be a reason or a trigger, but that isn't always the case.

Having a mental illness means you have to work harder, to push yourself to get through the day. It could be that you are trying to prevent yourself from feeling suicidal or trying to block out bad memories and thoughts. It can be very hard to fight against having these thoughts and feelings. Again, something else that may not be recognized by non-users. But this does show that there is strength there within, not weakness as is one of the stigmas around having a mental illness. Also, it's not always about being depressed or having anxiety. There are a lot of disorders in the mental health family and if everyone really dug deep within themselves, they would be able to relate to something within one or even more. We all have points in our lives where we feel we've had enough or can't cope anymore, or we've lost a loved one and it's traumatized us, and as we go through mourning, our mood worsens. We're only human and there are emotions that our brains don't know how to process, and this changes how your body and mind deals with the situation. I will say the stigma needs to be buried totally.

There's a lot of sacrifice made by those who suffer from a mental illness and the fact is, people don't think or even mention that side of it. I was a hardworking woman, but I lost my job, income, all that I had accomplished, loss of all the qualifications I worked so hard for, lost the high respect my colleagues had for me along with the social scene that I had with work colleagues.

I am a single mother of three. I feel guilty because I'm no longer the strong mother my kids knew. I feel like I failed my kids as a mother and role model, not being able to independently provide for them as I always had, the constant fear that they will look at me as though I am weak, that I've ruined their life, I've prevented them from doing what they want to do, they may be hiding me and my illness from their friends because they are ashamed.

People with mental illness are at risk of losing his or her home, because he or she no longer has a working income and benefits don't pay enough. You can't get another mortgage, some companies won't give you a mortgage if you've had mental illness, and your mortgage protection premium may be refused because of mental illness.

I could no longer drive because of the seizures. I had to get rid of my car, and totally lost my independence of getting out and about. I had a great social life but could no longer go out due to uncontrolled seizures and severe pain. One by one, I watched as the social contacts drifted away. The invitations stopped and so did the visits to see if I was okay. I had what I thought was a great relationship, but once I was diagnosed with a mental illness I was abandoned. Now I'm left with the fear of being alone for the rest of my life.

These are just some of the things that have happened to me since all this started in 2010. By 2011, more and more symptoms were developing and I had to stop working. People don't look at all the things you lose and how difficult it is for you to fight against this and find alternative ways to pay your bills and function. I've come across people who have lost it all before, and they have fallen apart, but that's acceptable and seen as normal. If you have a mental illness and you lose it, all they say is you gave up on yourself and it's your own fault because your head wasn't in the game. It's frustrating that people see mental illness as a weakness when in fact you have to be a very strong person to live with any form of mental illness because:

1. Every day you are fighting to make it to the next.

2. The hardest thing you have to do each day is get up or want to have the will to get up.

3. You may go day after day with no one to talk to.

4. You have to battle with discrimination in work and with the benefit system, which can lead to poverty and homelessness.

5. It is debilitating.

6. You have to face a world in which some people don't want be associated with someone who is suffering with a mental illness.

7. Being isolated is a battle within itself, but again it's not seen as a battle it's seen as self-infliction, but it's those around you that can cause the isolation.

8. You have to function as best as you can. Sometimes we function better than most who live without a mental illness, because at least with OCD we keep things orderly and clean. If we suffer from depression, we are able to feel empathy. Patience is a virtue, and we have to be patient because it's a long process to get into the system. Then once you're in it, you could be waiting years before therapy starts. This shows how strong we have to be. I know some who haven't been able to wait and who give up, but the majority don't.

We don't get a break from it either, it's there when we shut our eyes, it's there in our dreams, it's there when we wake up. There's no break in the chain. We live with this around the clock. There's no quick fix or instant cure, it's a long up and down process.

Our needs are neglected and ignored. In some cases, we're treated differently by doctors. Some care and are sincerely concerned, but others think you're an attention seeker. I've never had that but I know people, especially within the younger generation, that it has been said to, and not just by doctors but family, peers and teachers too.

We also have to battle if we have been wrongly diagnosed. This could have a major impact on our future. Those who have been wrongly diagnosed have an uphill struggle to rectify the damage, and there is no support. Perspectives about you change so you lose your social credibility. You become exposed, judged, and have to listen to people's attitudes toward you and how they have changed. All this adds to the vulnerability you are already feeling.

These are just some of the things we face every day. It's a lot harder than most people realize. I urge people to be more considerate and mindful of the challenges we live with.

*

CARRIE WORTHINGTON<br>Carrie was diagnosed with depression,<br>anxiety, and trichotillomania in 2000 at age 41

The biggest obstacle is the stigma when one speaks about mental illness. The ignorance is still very much real. I am still cautious in talking about my, or anyone else's, illness in the workplace. In my personal life, I am someone who has depressive and anxiety related symptoms. I am not ashamed, it is what I have, but some people are still very ignorant to the symptoms, recovery, and treatment. I believe people need to know that we are actually normal people with an illness. I have championed against people saying the words "crazy," "insane," and all the labels that the world does not realize is actually meaning someone's illness.

When I started with NAMI, the National Alliance of Mental Illness, ten years ago the statistics were one in six people would be affected by mental illness (either have it or know someone who lives with it). This year, it is one in three. I believe the figure has gone up substantially because people are actually admitting to having an illness, or having a family member with an illness.

I try to speak up, fight the stigma and keep up to date with the scientific studies that are coming out as they now have scans of the brain. They are starting to be able to physically see the effects of these illnesses and what can help, what really helps and how effective it is. I do not feel alone, or that I have to hide who I am. I don't have to hide the fact that sometimes I'm just not feeling well. I give myself the choice of just resting (if I know it's being caused by stress) or exercising or other activities that I need to do to stimulate or distract the thoughts. It's manageable with the proper treatment, knowledge and effort.

*

At the root of this dilemma is the way we view
mental health in this country. Whether an illness
affects your heart, your leg or your brain, it's
still an illness and there should be no distinction.
-MICHELLE OBAMA

*

CHAPTER SEVENTEEN

# Describing How It Feels

It's so common it could be anyone. The trouble is nobody wants to talk about it. And that makes everything worse. -RUBY WAX

Mental illness refers to a wide range of mental health disorders that affect our mood, thinking and behavior. Examples of mental illness include depression, anxiety disorders, schizophrenia, eating disorders, and addictive behaviors. Many people have mental health concerns from time to time, but not everyone has a mental illness. For those who don't understand, what is the best way to describe what it's like living with a mental illness?

\*

ADRIANNE ALLEN-LANG
Adrianne was diagnosed with dissociative
identity disorder in 2015 at age 18

It really depends on the person. For me, it's like being in an unpredictable horror movie every day, I don't know what's going to happen or how I'm going to react to things while being dissociated.

My mind is like being in a boxed room. There's a TV in each of the four corners playing different shows and music at different volumes, and you're trying to do the hardest cognitive exam while having a splitting migraine and widespread body pain.

Knowing what I know now, I wish someone had been more educated in the broader spectrum of mental illness to diagnose me sooner than I was at age eighteen. Mental illness has made a mess of my life. It's not a nice way to live your life but you've got to make the best of what you're given.

*

MORGAN BUTLER
Morgan was diagnosed with depression
and anxiety in 2009 at age 15

Living with mental illness is complicated to describe. I've had depression and anxiety for as long as I can remember. I have always felt things very deeply, to the point where my reactions to something small can be very deep for me. Emotion clouds logic, and usually my body reacts to the emotion that I am feeling. Feeling anxious about a test turns into heart pounding panic; feeling disappointed in an action I did or how it affected someone turns into a deeply rooted guilt and self-shame, that makes me feel physically heavy, and even sick.

The best resources I had outside of counseling, friends, and family was to go online and seek out others who feel the way I do. I am a huge supporter of the nonprofit "To Write Love on Her Arms," many bands and musicians rep their attire, and that's how I found out about them and their story. The suicide prevention hotline is 800-273-8255 (TALK) - you or a loved one could be in a crisis, just call. These people are on local lines trained to talk you through anything that depression and anxiety throws at you. Something I do now is talk to others on Reddit, but I need to know my limit on taking on others' problems. You can help others and help yourself at the same time, but you cannot pour from an empty glass.

\*

LYNDA CHELDELIN FELL
Lynda was diagnosed with depression in 2000 at age 35
and posttraumatic stress disorder in 2012 at age 47

The best way to describe a depressive episode is the feeling of being caught in a deep, dark hole. I feel utter hopelessness, like the technicolor has been robbed from my world and everything is gray. I can hear the birds singing but the beauty of the sound doesn't register in my brain. I can see the brilliant sunset, but nature's paintbrush fails to move me like it usually does. It's as if I can't hear or see anything. The worst part is that even if someone offered an outstretched hand to help me out of that hole, I wouldn't have energy to reach for it. It's a very scary feeling because it creates deep fear that beauty and hope will never return again. Without hope, we have nothing.

\*

SHAUNA COX
Shauna was diagnosed with an
anxiety disorder in 2009 at age 26

I think anyone with any kind of illness, mental or otherwise, struggles at times. For me, the anxiety disorder is almost a constant in my life. I am known by my friends as someone who stresses out a lot. My brain is constantly working, and often worrying nonstop about issues that others can forget within a minute of the worry coming into their head. New experiences, or old ones that have caused me anxiety in the past, bring the familiar and uncomfortable sensations of panic.

I get hot, sweaty, my heart races, my breathing becomes shallow, and I have diarrhea. These are embarrassing reactions in any situation, and adds to the stress which only serves to make it worse. I am also constantly overthinking and overanalyzing any social situation to the point where I find myself paralyzed with fear at making a fool of myself. As a result, I have missed out on a lot of fun times.

While I have progressed to the point that I am not always anxious anymore, and I can face situations that used to cause a wave of anxiety to rush over me, I am still not one hundred percent free of anxiety. I don't think anyone ever is, but in my case, because of the disorder it is that much harder for me to be rid of it. Whereas everyone feels anxiety at one point or another, for me it tends to last longer and hit harder.

It's difficult to live with a mental illness. Because it's not treated the same way as physical illnesses are, I think a lot of people (myself included) tend to sometimes feel embarrassed that they suffer with a mental illness. This can make it harder to seek out help, but I think it's important that people feel comfortable enough to ask for assistance when needed. Mental illness and seeking therapy need to be better accepted in today's society, so that when people do need mental help, they won't be afraid to seek it.

Had I known at the onset how helpful therapy would be, I would have sought help sooner. I think back to when I first went to a psychologist, and I wonder if my symptoms would have progressed as far, had I gone to a therapist as soon as I noticed that I had a problem.

It is amazing what a difference talking to a psychologist can make. Even just a couple of sessions into therapy, I felt better. I learned that I wasn't alone in what I was going through, and that there were strategies that existed that could make me feel better, and that could help me to fight through the anxiety I was experiencing. I felt a sense of relief after each therapy session, armed with new strategies I could use in my everyday life. While it's not an overnight fix, and some days are easier than others, therapy is a huge help for getting through any mental illness, and anxiety in particular. It is hard to feel like you are alone in your fight, and so to anyone fighting a mental illness, I urge you to find someone to talk to.

\*

JANE MCDONALD
Jane was diagnosed with major depressive disorder in 1989, multiple anxiety disorders in 2001, multiple personality disorders in 2007, and dissociative identity disorder in 2014

I experience my mental illness as a rollercoaster ride with ups, downs, twists and turns, peaks and valleys. The days when I am okay and feeling stable are the days when the rollercoaster is even-keel, running parallel to the ground. No peaks, no valleys. Other days, the rollercoaster plummets into a dark hole. Here it is cold, dark, and scary. I lack the motivation to do anything, I lack any joy or meaning in my life. The color fades from my life and everything becomes black and white. I am tired and feel alone and utterly helpless. All I can do, is go along with the ride and hope and pray for the times when I will hit a peak again and the rollercoaster will climb out of this pit that it has gone into. At times, I am in this dark pit for days, weeks, or even months, and there doesn't seem to be any end in sight. But eventually the roller coaster will start to climb again and I will emerge into the sunlight. Still other times, the rollercoaster turns sideways, does flips, or even goes backwards. Things are never as simple as good or bad, up or down. There are a whole host of other emotions that come into play, but they are all part of the same ride.

*

AMY OWEN
Amy was diagnosed with ADD and
bipolar disorder in 2014 at age 42

It is like having heart disease. I have a problem that requires medicine and self-improvement. I wish I had gone earlier to the doctor, or seen a doctor who diagnosed me correctly. Do not wait to get help. You aren't a broken person if you're diagnosed or get help for a mental illness. You can lead a normal life. It is better than making mistake after mistake.

*

DENISE PURCELL
Denise was diagnosed with depression, posttraumatic stress
disorder, and dissociative identity disorder in 1995 at age 30

That there are a lot of mental illnesses, and most likely they end up knowing someone either in family or friends who have one. It's nothing to segregate yourself from. A lot of times they are under medication and/or therapy for the illness. It's not any different than having a medical disorder. You would go and have that diagnosed, researched, and decide the best avenue for your well-being. That's the same for mental illness. There is never the need for ignorance on any level. There's too much information out there at the tip of your finger.

*

ERICKA REEVE
Ericka was diagnosed with dissociative identity disorder,
posttraumatic stress disorder, obsessive-compulsive disorder,
depression, anxiety and an eating disorder in 2013 at age 26

The best way to describe my life is like driving a car. All is well and good, and suddenly it's five months later and you find yourself at the beach. It feels dream-like, almost a dizziness and floating. And it depends on the part. It's like driving a car, and kids or other passengers are constantly arguing or asking repeated questions like "Are we there yet?" There's playing and then crying, singing and then screaming. Trying to speak and no words come out. It can be terrifying, but now I find comfort in even my most vocal and protective parts. As a collective, we very much want people to understand that we spent my life simply trying to survive. We are not dangerous or evil or crazy. I, and we, want to live. We are no longer satisfied with the bare minimum of survival. Now, we want to actually live.

\*

LORRAINE SCOTT
Lorraine was diagnosed with non-epilepsy attack disorder
and dissociative identity disorder in 2016 at age 48

Learning that I had a mental illness or two was a lot to take in. Although on one hand you're relieved that you have a diagnosis for the way you been feeling and all the symptoms you have been enduring now have some meaning. Once those thoughts went through and were weighing down my brain even more, as reality is kicking in you start to think about others and how are they going to take it, will I get support, will I be frowned upon? It goes on and on, and I think the biggest fear for me was what impact this was going to have on my relations with others.

It's by far one of the hardest illnesses anyone will ever have to deal with because of the stigma, especially with the older generations. It seems to be more acceptable within the younger generation, and you aren't frowned upon and it's accepted by them. My main support network is from my kids and their friends. All of them are below twenty-seven years of age. I also have a couple friends that I went to school with who have given me a lot of support.

Thank you to you all for being there and giving me the love and support to get through each day, you all know who you are and I love you all to bits.

These people help by either popping in to make me a coffee, or inviting me out to catch up, or coming and helping with my chores. When they wipe away my tears, give me a hug, send me a message, buy me flowers or other gifts and, in some cases, just being by my side, they give me hope by showing me that they want me to get better and will be by my side all the way. The little things matter and it all helps towards getting better.

The other week, one of my long-time friends from secondary school came to see me and brought flowers and cheesecake. Both of these put a smile on my face, and perked me up so much. Now I'm not saying that bringing me something is important, it was the fact that she did something to cheer me up. It didn't just cheer me up, it made me feel valued by someone other than my children.

My life has changed tremendously and not by my own doing. A lot of my illness was caused by the aftermath of many traumas. I've always been a nice person who would help anyone I can. If I can't help, I will listen and give them the chance to talk to get things off their chest. It's not always easy because it could trigger bad memories for me, but I wouldn't let that be known and I would let them carry on. I try to give good advice that may be helpful within their situation.

The truth is, if you love someone who has been diagnosed with a mental illness, trust me when I say they need people to be there. Support and listen to them, not just to what's gone on or is going on.

Listen mainly about how they are feeling. Each day they will have different thoughts that fight each other, so it's good for them to know that someone truly cares and is there for them. We all need a safe network of people. This could be just one person or it could be a few people we trust and know will be there.

It's far from easy for us and for our support network, but it's important to have this in place. It's frightening for people with mental illness to hear that no one wants to know, or be told that there's nothing wrong with them, and they're just an attention seeker, or crazy, or it's all in their head. We don't need that; we just want to get better. But when society makes us feel that it's not acceptable to have a mental illness, then what hope is there for us getting better?

I've always been a very strong woman, even at my weakest I'm still strong. My weakness is kept hidden behind closed doors, or was. I very rarely give up on anything, and I have spent my life fighting to survive. I feel that I have been successful through life, and I've had a mental illness since the young age of five. That's when all the traumas started and I would imagine being someone else. I've managed to get to age forty-eight before being diagnosed. I've lived a normal life. I married, had kids, worked, owned a car, a home, enjoyed holidays, and a social life, etc. I had it all and no one knew anything. Even though I had moments that I questioned at times, I never thought I had a mental illness. I would also say to others:

- Don't give up, there is help out there. It may take a while but there is light at the end of the tunnel.

- Seek help immediately. Don't leave it too long, because it can be a lengthy process anyway.

- Keep on at your doctor, and see them regularly, so they can keep a log on the system of how you're coping or not coping.

- Organize a safe place, but try and avoid the bedroom.

- Organize a safe network of people you trust and you know want to support you through this.

- Try and find something you enjoy doing to distract your mind from negative issues. Get a hobby to keep the mind positively active.

- Try and talk with someone every day, it doesn't have to be face to face, it could just be messaging or a phone call. This helps you feel connected to the outside world in some way.

- Each week, treat yourself to something. It can be anything from a bar of chocolate, out for a coffee, a walk, a day or night out with friends, something you've been saving for, etc.

- Do grounding and relaxation techniques. These can be found on the internet or from therapy sessions.

This is what I do to keep me going, and I have positive days and I have negative days, but I'm now more on the positive side than negative. Three months ago, I was on the negative side more than positive, so this has helped me tremendously.

*

CARRIE WORTHINGTON
Carrie was diagnosed with depression,
anxiety, and trichotillomania in 2000 at age 41

Most of the time, and especially after years of having depression and anxiety, I can recognize when things just aren't right. Today, I can manage my life around my illness. Sometimes I lay low during the weekend. I find things to do around the house, and try to not see a lot of people when I'm just not feeling well. If I'm feeling anxious or depressed, I try to make sure I exercise, eat right, and get enough sleep. These are all very important to give me the best shot of not having any low or anxious times.

The extreme grief I've experienced in the past five years has put a huge strain on my ability to take care of myself. However, because of the grief, I have been through a lot of therapy. At this point, I have learned to be aware of thoughts that can weigh me down. I have been able to learn how to turn it around, change thoughts, do activities and other things to assist myself in managing and moving forward. The most important thing to know is that I'm no different from anyone else. I have an illness; it is who I am. I am actively and consciously managing it and doing the best I can. Sometimes, no matter what I try, I'm going to have the symptoms that go with anxiety and depression. I have to do what I need to do to get through it. Most of the time, not many people are aware of this.

What people have to understand is that mental illness cannot just be turned off. The idea of being told to be happy or calm down is ridiculous. When speaking about mental illness, stigma and the insensitivity, I always frame the words with another disease. You wouldn't tell someone with rheumatoid arthritis or multiple sclerosis to just walk it out. It usually makes a point that mental illness is not a feeling or emotions that can be controlled.

There are medications and tools that can help control symptoms, but like every other illness, it is not something people can just stop doing. Also like other illnesses, there are several different types of treatments, and a person has to choose what is best for them. Unfortunately, unlike other illness, there is not a test, blood work, or even any kind of digital scan to diagnose and treat. Everyone is unique and it is a difficult and slow process to find out the exact coverage and medication that will help someone.

*

CHAPTER EIGHTEEN

# *Importance of Hope*

Be like the birds, sing after every storm.
-BETH MENDE CONNY

Hope is the fuel that propels us forward, urges us to get out of bed each morning. It is the promise that tomorrow will be better than today. Living with mental illness can redefine our hope in unexpected ways. What does hope mean to you today?

\*

ADRIANNE ALLEN-LANG
Adrianne was diagnosed with dissociative
identity disorder in 2015 at age 18

Waking up to my son's beautiful smile every day and knowing that no matter what, I have someone who loves and needs me.

\*

MORGAN BUTLER
Morgan was diagnosed with depression
and anxiety in 2009 at age 15

Hope is such a complex, yet simple concept. Having depression and anxiety can make it very difficult to enjoy some of life's simplicities. When you have an up day, or a moment of clarity, sometimes something as simple as a smile from a child, or the sun peeking through from behind some trees, or seeing a heads-up penny on the ground—those things are incredible.

Hope is realizing that mental illness gives temporary limitations on our feelings and capabilities. Even though it's something you live with, you can do just that: live. You don't need to survive your illness. You can dominate it with the right tools, support system, and mindset. It's hard and it's a cycle, but it's always beatable. When you live with mental illness, you understand others with it. When you have it in check, you can begin to pour from your glass and invest into helping others feel like they aren't alone. Maybe I have anxiety and depression so that I can help others like me. Hope is real. Hope is infinite. Hope is a light that can be found in the darkest of places. Hope can be shared.

*

LYNDA CHELDELIN FELL
Lynda was diagnosed with depression in 2000 at age 35<br>and posttraumatic stress disorder in 2012 at age 47

If you had asked me this question before losing my daughter and my husband's stroke, my answer would be much different. Before tragedy struck, I hoped my children would get into the college of their choice or have a good job. What I saw as barriers or challenges before, are now seen as opportunities for growth. We never grow from the easy stuff; that is simply how life is. Now, hope holds a very different meaning for me. It has become the fuel that gets me up every morning. Hope is nourishment for my soul that life is worth living. I have so much more appreciation for life and compassion for people.

So hope now looks much different than it did before the accident and my husband's stroke. I no longer hope for tangible things. Rather I hope for things such as peace, gratitude, and love. I know what life without hope looks and feels like. I worked hard to create hope in my life once again. So now hope is what I aspire to give other people, because in doing so it helps my own heart to heal.

\*

SHAUNA COX
Shauna was diagnosed with an
anxiety disorder in 2009 at age 26

My definition of hope when it comes to mental illness is not only a desire to get better, but also an expectation that I will succeed in completely overcoming my anxiety disorder in the future.

Before finding help, fighting a mental illness can seem hopeless. It can feel like you are going to be suffering with your affliction for the rest of your life. I am an example of someone who was in the depths of an anxiety disorder, found help in the form of a therapist, medication, and the support of loved ones, and crawled my way out. It is possible to get better, and it is possible to overcome illness. It is important that one never gives up hope and that one always looks to the future possibilities.

Fighting an anxiety disorder has shown me that there are people in my life that I can depend on. It has made me see just how lucky I am to have my husband, Roger, in my life. I know that I would have eventually succeeded in fighting this if he weren't in my life, but I also know that it would have been a lot harder without him. I think to the times where he has been there supporting me through anxiety attacks, and to the moments when he has helped me face uncomfortable social situations that have ended in me having fun despite my fears, and I realize that he is a huge thing in my life to be thankful for.

Having an anxiety disorder has also helped me to be more compassionate and understanding toward others fighting a similar battle, whether it be with anxiety or any other mental illness. With my psychology background, I've always had a soft spot for people with mental illness. But actually going through one myself has given me greater insight and more perspective into understanding people with similar problems.

\*

JANE MCDONALD
Jane was diagnosed with major depressive disorder in 1989,
multiple anxiety disorders in 2001, multiple personality
disorders in 2007, and dissociative identity disorder in 2014

For me, hope means that even on the darkest, most difficult days, even when I am completely exhausted and ready to give up, I still fight the good fight. It means struggling and believing that things will get better. I know there is no cure for my mental illnesses. Even my psychiatrist has admitted that I will always have really bad days. But there will also be better days and eventually over time and with lots of therapy, the good days may outweigh the bad ones.

Hope means that even when I want to stay inside and hide under the covers, I still get up and go outside when I can. It means getting out of bed, showering, and getting dressed, even when I just want to sleep all day long. It means going to my art group, visiting or calling friends, and doing other things that I may not have been able to just a day ago, a week ago, or a month ago. It means recognizing that I may not be able to do those things again in a day, a week, or a month, but that I still try. It means knowing things will never be perfect, that I will always have mental illness, but that I can manage it.

Part of hope for me is getting involved in advocacy and speaking out on behalf of those with mental illness and other challenges who cannot advocate for themselves. It means recognizing even the smallest of achievements, and believing that those small things will lead to larger and larger accomplishments. Hope means believing that I will find a medication combination that can help me manage my symptoms without horrendous side effects.

Hope means continuing to struggle, continuing to fight, even though I am ready to give up at times. It means believing that the struggle will get easier eventually.

*

AMY OWEN
Amy was diagnosed with ADD and
bipolar disorder in 2014 at age 42

Hope is not giving up. It means you have faith in yourself and God. Hope is your best asset in getting through your illness. Hope is a beautiful thing.

*

DENISE PURCELL
Denise was diagnosed with depression, posttraumatic stress
disorder, and dissociative identity disorder in 1995 at age 30

Hope is a possibility, always a chance. Now for me, that doesn't mean there's a cure for my mental illness. It means for me, there is a chance for people to better understand and accept me for who I am. Just like everyone else in this world, if you can see beyond the label, you might end up with the most loyal, caring friend or family you ever had. I hope that one day there might be less mental illnesses that are caused by other people, such as PTSD and dissociative identity disorder. We are not bad people, we are just living differently. We view differently. We are far from broken and don't need fixing.

*

LORRAINE SCOTT
Lorraine was diagnosed with non-epilepsy attack disorder
and dissociative identity disorder in 2016 at age 48

My hope is my family and my family is my hope.

My hope is the soul of my future.

My hope is waking up each morning feeling positive about what the day will bring.

My hope is the engine that is revved when I'm down to drive me back up to the purls of happiness.

My hope is to never give up on myself or life.

My hope is defeating my fears.

My hope is seeing the light erase the dark.

My hope is not to judge and not be judged.

My hope is to look at the face of my enemy and smile

My hope is the vision I now have on life…Live it to the maximum.

My hope is to forgive those who do me wrong.

My hope is to provide happiness to those most in need of it.

My hope is to give, to help, to console.

My hope is to help those who feel weak to become strong.

My hope is to see the positives even where none exist.

I see myself as a different and even stronger person than ever before, I've learned so much about me that I didn't know, and with this I'm content with who I am. I look for the positives, I try to inspire others.

I want to help myself get better and deal with the issues that have caused struggles in my life. It's time for me to face these so that I can move forward with my life instead of being held back by the past. Choosing to write my stories is helping with the process of opening up and facing the traumas of my past.

For once in my life I can say, I love me. The reason this is so big to me is because I've spent my life feeling or thinking that I wasn't loved. All I wanted was for someone to love and want me, but the fact was I didn't even love me and didn't even know what love was or how it felt. Love struck me when I lost my first baby, and there is no end to the love I have for my children and grandchildren. From being able to give love I have learned to love myself and I no longer seek the approval or love of others.

I hope that one day I will be standing in front of groups giving inspirational talks on various subjects in which I have true life experiences.

*

CARRIE WORTHINGTON
Carrie was diagnosed with depression,
anxiety, and trichotillomania in 2000 at age 41

My definition of hope is to want to look forward to a life of joy. It has been very difficult, until about a year ago, to even imagine I could have that at all. Before that, right after my husband passed, I had such dark moments, ending up in the hospital a few times and not having any hope for any type of life. I have worked really hard to get where I am today, learning about things I've suppressed for most of my life, how I can pull myself down (no need for any outside influences, I can do it all by myself), and how I can use several practices (mindfulness, turning negative thoughts into positive, not taking everything that is happening personal, etc.) to get through the day.

I no longer feel like life is hopeless, that I can't move on, that life is impossible. I have come out of despair and darkness. I have survived, and I can recognize now that I did. Sometimes I have to remind myself that I did do it, and continue to recognize the good, happy and strong things I've done. I have been successful in handling one day at a time in a positive and hopeful manner. I am now working on seeing my future as a widow, accepting my life, and reinventing my future plans and how that looks.

*

CHAPTER NINETEEN

# Making Peace with our Journey

I don't want my pain and struggle to make me a
victim. I want my battle to make me someone else's
hero. -ANONYMOUS

Every journey is as unique as one's fingerprint, for we experience different beliefs, desires, needs, and we often walk different roads. Though we may not see anyone else on the path, we are never truly alone, for more walk behind, beside, and in front of us. In this chapter lies the answers to the final question posed to the writers: What would you like the world to know about your mental illness journey?

\*

ADRIANNE ALLEN-LANG
Adrianne was diagnosed with dissociative
identity disorder in 2015 at age 18

I'd like to let the world know that we are not our diagnosis. We are not monsters, and we have so much to give. Please look over our flaws and see the love and passion we have to give.

*

MORGAN BUTLER
Morgan was diagnosed with depression
and anxiety in 2009 at age 15

Mental illness may be a part of you, but it doesn't define you. Know that there are so many resources and so much love, hope, and beauty in this world to be shared.

I have anxiety and depression, but I don't live a life defined by it. I must be open about this facet of my life in order to be authentic, and in order to surround myself by true, compassionate people, I must be open to letting them help me, and be there for them.

Whatever you're going through, you can get through it, and there are people who want to help you along the way.

*

LYNDA CHELDELIN FELL
Lynda was diagnosed with depression in 2000 at age 35
and posttraumatic stress disorder in 2012 at age 47

I want the world to know that mental illness is no different than any other medical disease. It is nondiscriminatory, and can affect anyone. Sadly, many who live with mental illness either don't know it or are lost between the cracks of society. It's important that we work to remove the stigma so those affected by mental illness don't hide like my great-grandmother did.

By coming out and sharing my story, I want the world to know that living with mental illness has no impact upon our intelligence and ability to be loving, compassionate, contributing members of society. Many historic figures including Abraham Lincoln and Isaac Newton lived with mental illness. In today's world, Carrie Fisher, Elton John, and Catherine Zeta-Jones are but a few celebrities known to live with mental illness. I want the world to know that people who live with mental illness can find the support and treatment they need to lead a rich, fulfilling life. Let's not let stigma stop them from doing that.

*

SHAUNA COX
Shauna was diagnosed with an
anxiety disorder in 2009 at age 26

I think it's important to realize that mental illness doesn't just go away. Medication or therapy are often needed and can help greatly. However, I have experienced that there are often ups and downs when dealing with a mental illness. While I have improved significantly since I first sought out help in therapy, there are still tough days. There are still times when I feel the anxiety rush in, and I am brought almost back to the beginning. While it tends to be bad for a short amount of time rather than every day, all day, it is still something that is there, lurking in the background.

I am not completely free of the anxiety, and I don't know if I ever will be. It is still hard for me to be in a big social group, like a party, and I am guilty of avoiding them whenever possible. I still have panic like moments when I feel myself getting hot and need to run to the bathroom. If Roger is late coming home, I still sometimes worry that something bad has happened to him. I also worry on a regular basis that I will lose him at a young age, and maybe because it is my biggest fear, it is hard for me to let go of that anxiety completely.

When I am heading to the airport or to a large shopping center with hard-to-find bathrooms, I will take an anxiolytic in preparation for the anxiety that is still at times hard to fight. I am, however, much better than I once was. I can feel a panic attack coming, and I can often talk my way through it. I will say my mantra, and then put all of my energy into focusing on anything other than the anxiety, and other than whatever is triggering the anxiety. I am getting better at this, and there are more and more times when something that would have been a trigger in the past isn't anymore. The other day, I went grocery shopping by myself, and a brief thought of, "What if I need to go to the bathroom?" entered my mind. The thought was gone as quickly as it came, and I continued on with my trip. While I know that the anxiety is separate from who I am as a person, I'm not rid of it yet, and will continue to work to better myself so hopefully, at some point in the near future, none of my decisions will be motivated by anxiety provoked thoughts or fears.

People fighting mental illnesses are incredibly brave. They are often courageous in sharing their experience with others, and in continuing to live and fight every day. I think that others can learn from those living with a mental illness. It takes determination, bravery, hard work and persistence. In succeeding to fight any mental illness, it makes us people who others can and should learn from. We have been to the bottom and managed to climb our way out with valuable life lessons along the way.

*

JANE MCDONALD
Jane was diagnosed with major depressive disorder in 1989,
multiple anxiety disorders in 2001, multiple personality
disorders in 2007, and dissociative identity disorder in 2014

There are so many things that I wish people knew about living with mental illness. Perhaps the most important for me is that living with mental illness is not a choice, and it is not our fault. Having a mental illness is no different than having cancer or diabetes or Parkinson's. We do not choose to have a mental illness. Many times there are biochemical reasons for our illnesses. Other times they emerge because of unhealthy environments and circumstances that we have had to live in or endure. Mental illness is never the person's fault. We do not like having mental illness, and if we had our way we would be completely healthy. No one wants to be mentally ill, just as no one wants to have cancer or dementia. It just happens to people.

Also along these lines, I want people to understand that you can't wish the illness away any more than wishful thinking can eliminate any other illness. It takes hard work and a lot of strength to live with a mental illness and we cannot simply fix it with positive thinking. Often times, we are trying everything we can to make life better, but it is a real struggle and having people tell us to get over it, think positively, or other such things can be very invalidating and hurtful.

I also want people to know that we do not mean to hurt you or your feelings if we say or do something wrong. If I isolate and do not call or text you, it is often because I am feeling extremely depressed and hiding in my bed trying to sleep so I don't feel my profound sadness. I do not repeatedly turn down invitations because I'm being rude. I am struggling with social anxiety and find that leaving my apartment and being in social situations is very anxiety provoking and stressful.

It is not that I do not want to be with you or my other friends, it is just too difficult for me to do right now. That doesn't mean I want you to abandon me though. I depend upon and value your love and support more than you know. Often knowing I have people like you in my life is all that gets me through the day.

I wish people knew that those with mental illness want to just be listened to sometimes. We don't want you to give us advice or to fix our problems. We just want you to be there, to be a shoulder to cry on, or a listening ear to hear us out. Often times, you don't even have to say anything at all. Just being there helps. At the same time, however, sometimes we need to be alone and would appreciate it if you could respect that. We all need alone time now and then, and people with certain mental illness just may need more time alone than others.

I also would like people to know that we experience the same emotions as you but that we often feel them differently. We all feel sad, anxious, scared, surprised, or uncertain at times. It's just that sometimes those with mental illness, particularly those with personality disorders such as myself, feel all of these emotions much more intensely and have a difficult time regulating them. We may feel all of these things, and more, all at once and can easily become overwhelmed by it all.

I would also like to clear up a few stereotypes and myths. Primarily, that we are not "doing this" for the attention. We do not like having mental illness. Trust me, no one wants mental illness any more than they want to have a stroke or heart disease. We may "act out" at times, but this is because we are often in a lot of emotional pain and do not know how else to deal with it. In high school, I often felt suicidal and either made suicide attempts or engaged in self-harm. The last thing someone who is in this state needs to hear from a professional, a friend, a family member, or anyone else is that they are doing it for the attention. We are in pain. We are doing it because that is how we cope. That is how we deal with our pain.

Other misconceptions abound that we are lazy, weak, and worthless. People think we are incapable of making a contribution to society, but that is far from truth. Studies have shown that when people with mental illness are given the right opportunities, they often enjoy working and volunteering in their communities, and they make valuable contributions. We may need some additional support, but we are more than able to be productive, contributing members of society. And we want to help. We want to contribute. No one likes lying around in bed all day.

I would also like to point out that things are not always as they seem and that many people who you see smiling and laughing are often suffering from depression, anxiety, or other mental illness. In Canada alone, it is estimated that one in five people suffer from a mental illness. We are everywhere. We are your mother, father, brother, sister, aunt, uncle, cousin, coworker, friend, neighbor. We may look like we have it all together, but that is because we have learned to keep up appearances. We learn that to avoid stigma and being ostracized, we must appear "normal." Meanwhile, underneath that façade, we are struggling, we are fighting, and we are hurting. But we are trying our best.

Finally, I want people to know to please not give up on us. It may not look like we are doing much or are making much of a contribution to society, but we are doing our best. Having a mental illness is like fighting a battle every day of your life. Sometimes you lose, sometimes you win, and the next day you get up and do it all over again. If we are tired and sad and anxious, it is because we are often caught in this war against mental illness. Please do not give up on us. We are doing our absolute best.

\*

AMY OWEN
Amy was diagnosed with ADD and
bipolar disorder in 2014 at age 42

This book, *Living with Mental Illness*, is important and difficult. It's a real issue that needs to be taken seriously by the medical community. The stigma needs to go away.

\*

DENISE PURCELL
Denise was diagnosed with depression, posttraumatic stress disorder, and dissociative identity disorder in 1995 at age 30

That it's real and difficult and exhausting. There are normal everyday things in life that we are expected to take care of. Having a mental illness on top of that is really hard to handle at times, and we shouldn't be made to feel unimportant, ashamed, ousted from society. We are doing the best we can with what we have. So maybe we need more therapy or understanding—no one is perfect. Just because we look normal on the outside doesn't mean we are not struggling on the inside. Be patient, loving and understanding, or decide not to get involved with us. The choice is ultimately yours. But it's cruel to pretend in any form with someone with a mental illness.

\*

ERICKA REEVE
Ericka was diagnosed with dissociative identity disorder, posttraumatic stress disorder, obsessive-compulsive disorder, depression, anxiety and an eating disorder in 2013 at age 26

Living with my disorders, especially DID, can be terrifying, unnerving, horrific, silly, loud, enjoyable (at times), and exceptionally lonely. People with DID, people like us, live with each other. We're very different people in most instances, but we want to live as people, meaning that we want acknowledgment and respect. We are not freaks, and we're not evil or malicious. Mischievous, you bet, but we do seek out interactions with no intent to harm.

We want to be able to live our life, our lives, and we want understanding and acceptance when possible. I want people to know that my parts *are not* demon possession. Religion is part of our trauma, and it shouldn't have been that way. My life did not need to become *our* life, and it sure as s*** didn't need to become what it was.

We want people to realize that some of my parts are exceptionally talented writers (not so much the case for me, so I apologize, lol). Others are amazing at watercolor painting, some excel in math, and others have studied world religions to protect and gain information. Additionally, DID at its core is about survival. All of us, including everyone in this book, did that—we survived. Now I would imagine that we very much want to live.

"Normal is illusion. What is normal for the spider is chaos for the fly." —Morticia Addams. This quote has stuck with us for a very long time. I want to find my own definition of normal. DID isn't fun when you have no idea what is happening and why. It is not a joke, a Halloween costume, or make-believe. It comes along with many other disorders in many instances. My parts struggle with some of their own individual health problems. We want people to know that basic human kindness goes a long, long way. If you or someone you know or care about is struggling, be there without judgment. Someone asking why when we were young could have drastically altered my life for the better. If you see something, say something, and just be there.

\*

LORRAINE SCOTT
Lorraine was diagnosed with non-epilepsy attack disorder
and dissociative identity disorder in 2016 at age 48

Although it may be a shock to some or most of the people who know me, I found out in May 2016 that I had been living with a mental illness that could go back as far as the age of five years old due to the traumas that I had experienced from such a young age. Although it was a massive shock to me and my close ones, it's also given me the ability to understand me.

Everyone who has been in my life from friends, colleagues, schoolers, family, ex partners, parents and my kids have been around me not knowing that I had a mental illness or two, even I didn't know. The Lorraine you all know is still there and many of you won't ever see a different one. Some of my family members have seen a difference and wondered, but it's been nothing bad, other than how feisty I can be. In the past year of being diagnosed, it's taken some getting used to, and having to deal with it on my own with just my children has been very difficult and traumatic for us all. I've feared telling people of my illnesses because of how they may receive it and judge me, or stigmatize me. It's awful, when you think about people who you've grown up with or known for life as such, but you fear the way they think of you, even though you've never judged them and been nothing but nice to them. Unfortunately, with mental illness it is the stigma, and rather than educating themselves on an individual illness, you are judged on mental illness. Now as shocking as it may seem, please don't judge me, or think that I am weak, because it's far from the truth. I've always been a strong person and always will be no matter what's going on with me.

I have had to go day after day reliving the traumas, and I keep smiling even when feeling broken and traumatized inside. This is how I've gotten through life—by smiling, pretending to be happy, helping others constantly so I don't have to focus on my traumas. I've done this for forty-plus years. My life has been fighting the memories of these traumas and while doing that, I'm still being mom. I'm being a wife or partner, being a sister, daughter and a good friend helping others when and as needed with their own problems, working and so on. It all comes natural to me, being there for others and holding them up when my own traumas are tearing me apart.

I spent my life being selfless due to my love of seeing others happy and smiling. It was easy to forgive minor he-said-she-said gossip as some of the traumas I was fighting were far worse than someone gossiping about me. I never had time for gossip, to be fair, and so I would ignore it. If someone did upset me, I would dust myself off and carry on. Now I've learned why I was able to be like this.

My mental illnesses are non-epileptic attack disorder (NEAD), and dissociative identity disorder (DID).

NEAD is similar to epileptic seizures, but they are not caused by abnormal electrical activity in the brain (epileptic activity). Like epileptic seizures, NEAs can cause blacking out, collapsing, injuries and other seizure effects. Non-epileptic attack disorder (NEAD) occurs in around two to three people in every ten thousand. This means that in a typical town with three hundred thousand people, there are sixty to ninety who have NEAD in the UK.

Dissociative identity disorder, previously known as multiple personality disorder, is a severe condition in which two or more distinct identities, or personality states, are present in—and alternately take control of—an individual. The person also experiences memory loss that is too extensive to be explained by ordinary forgetfulness. It is thought to be a complex psychological condition that is likely caused by many factors, including severe trauma during early childhood (usually extreme, repetitive abuse).

Dissociative identity disorder is a severe form of dissociation, a mental process which produces a lack of connection in a person's thoughts, memories, feelings, actions, or sense of identity. Dissociative identity disorder is thought to stem from a combination of factors that may include trauma experienced by the person with the disorder. The dissociative aspect is thought to be a coping mechanism. Dissociation is one way the mind copes with too much stress, such as during a traumatic event.

I was having seizures all the time as a child, but now I know that they are stress related and that any form of stress from mental to physical stress will trigger a seizure, conk out, and blackout. This all came with vengeance in 2011. This is just my body and mind telling me it can't cope with whatever I'm doing, it could be as simple as sitting watching TV, it can trigger one off. With the dissociation, I know have a few characters depending on what is going on. So, if I'm being threatened, the strongest will come to the forefront to protect me by dealing with it, and she will stay up front until the threat is gone and she feels that I'm safe again. That's my way of explaining it.

Now you know about some of what I have been living with. I've made my difficult traumatic life look so simple. I can't do anything about what's happened to me in the past, but I can do something about my future and my first steps are writing about my experiences to start the healing process of coming to terms with my experiences.

\*

CARRIE WORTHINGTON
Carrie was diagnosed with depression,
anxiety, and trichotillomania in 2000 at age 41

I have worked very hard for over twenty years to stop the stigma associated with mental illness. In those early years I was told horrible things about my husband because he looked okay by people who just didn't understand. I saw the looks people gave him when he was too loud or too manic and was erratic. I know the groups of friends or families who stopped inviting us to things because he was embarrassing.

It has come a long way, but there is still stigma, especially from those who have not yet had their life touched by it, either to themselves or a close family member. More education is needed. I always ask people if they would slight people with diabetes or cancer. We need more education, treatment and availability of prevention in schools and helping young people learn to deal with life, which for some children is dramatically hard, and they are subject to a lot at a young age.

I am someone who has anxiety and depression. I don't believe I will ever not have it, but I do believe that it will not be the focus of my life. I don't believe it will be the catalyst that controls my life, I am confident that I will be able to control it. I've been taught strategies and how to keep it in check. Most times these days, there is no anxiety and I get through every day without any feelings of doubt, sadness or despair. I have learned I can grieve my husband's passing, but not have that overtake my life, my daily activities. I have a normal life. It is normal because it is who I am. Some people might look at my life, the life I've had and what I've done, what I've dealt with when my husband was alive and in the throes of mental illness and never think, at least to them, that it is normal. Today, I am more than aware of what is going on, how to recognize it and acknowledge it, and then how to get through with little or no effect on my life and moving forward. I have spent the past twenty years fighting against the stigma against mental illness. It is very hard for people to deal with, both having it and being around it. Illnesses of the mind are not visible, therefore some cannot understand or believe it is not the person but the illness. That is why I've fought for awareness of what mental illness is, to stop discrimination, promote research and most of all, acceptance.

*

CHAPTER TWENTY

# Meet the writers

\*

ADRIANNE ALLEN-LANG
Adrianne was diagnosed with dissociative
identity disorder in 2015 at age 18

Adrianne Allen-Lang was born in a small town in New South Wales, Australia. Her parents split when she was two years old, and then her mother moved her and her younger brother to the city when Adrianne was five. After moving fourteen hours away at age fourteen to escape abuse, Adrianne became pregnant at age fifteen by an abusive man. She gave birth to her son at age sixteen in 2014, all on her own. She is now eighteen years old and after a five-year hiatus, is restarting school to gain her diploma.

\*

MORGAN BUTLER
Morgan was diagnosed with depression
and anxiety in 2009 at age 15

Morgan Butler was born and raised in the Pacific Northwest. She earned her Bachelor of Arts in Art and Design from the University of Washington in 2016. She currently works in Marketing and Graphic Design, and spends much of her time creating, crafting, and spending time with her dog and family.

\*

LYNDA CHELDELIN FELL
Lynda was diagnosed with depression in 2000 at age 35
and posttraumatic stress disorder in 2012 at age 47

Born and raised in the Pacific Northwest, when Lynda Cheldelin Fell met Australian-born Jamie, it was love at first sight and they married nine months later. They happily raised four children in Lynda's hometown, where they were surrounded by love and support when Lynda and Jamie's fifteen-year-old daughter, Aly, died in a car accident in 2009. Just when Lynda thought life couldn't get any worse, it did. Her beloved forty-six-year-old husband Jamie buried his head (and grief) in the sand. He escaped into eighty-hour work weeks, more wine, more food, and less talking. His blood pressure shot up, his cholesterol went off the chart, and the perfect storm arrived on June 4, 2012. Suddenly, Lynda's beloved began drooling and couldn't speak; he was having a major stroke. Somewhere in the fog, Lynda was diagnosed with posttraumatic stress disorder but her depression began years before, after her hysterectomy at age thirty-five. Raised in a culture where depression and mental illness were taboo to discuss, Lynda is dedicated to raising awareness and helping others who share her path feel less alone.

*

SHELBY COLICH JOHNSON
Shelby was diagnosed with
depression in 2005 at age 12

The second of four children, Shelby was born in Indianapolis, Indiana in July 1992. After graduating high school in 2011, she began her college journey to pursue a degree in Elementary Education, but after three semesters, put those plans on hold which provided the necessary time to reevaluate her career goals and put life in perspective.

\*

SHAUNA COX
Shauna was diagnosed with an
anxiety disorder in 2009 at age 26

Shauna Cox was born in Montreal and moved to Toronto at age thirteen. She later graduated with a specialized honors bachelor's degree in psychology and a post-graduate certificate in autism and behavioral sciences. Shortly after meeting her future husband, Roger, she moved to St. Paul, Alberta. She currently works as a receptionist at a veterinary clinic which is perfect for her love of animals, but also dreams of one day writing and publishing a novel. Shauna and Roger also have dreams of having children, but in the meantime they are putting all of their attention into their three fur-babies: Riley and Roxey (two Jack Russell Terriers), and PussyBear (their cat). In her spare time, Shauna enjoys camping, hiking, traveling, reading and writing.

\*

JANE MCDONALD

Jane was diagnosed with major depressive disorder in 1989,
multiple anxiety disorders in 2001, multiple personality
disorders in 2007, and dissociative identity disorder in 2014

Jane was born and raised in the suburbs of a major Canadian city. She is the youngest of two children and grew up in a divorced home with her mother and sister. Jane's struggles with mental illness began at a young age but went undiagnosed for many years. At age ten, she was diagnosed with major depressive disorder. She struggled through high school and later went on to university, during which time she was further diagnosed with PTSD, general anxiety disorder, social anxiety disorder, and several phobias. Jane eventually graduated with an Honors B.A. in psychology and anthropology. She was later diagnosed with three personality disorders and, recently, with dissociative identity disorder. Jane is passionate about animals and has been a mother to her fur-baby Alex for the past twelve years until his recent passing. She volunteers with a local mental health organization where she strives to advocate for those with mental health issues and combat the stigma around such illnesses. She has also served as chair of a Tenant Board and advocates for those living in poverty and on social assistance.

\*

AMY OWEN
Amy was diagnosed with ADD and
bipolar disorder in 2014 at age 42

Amy Owen was raised in Wheaton, Illinois and Plano, Texas. She earned her B.A. in exercise physiology. After college, she moved with friends to Hilton Head Island, South Carolina. There, she met her first husband. They moved back to Illinois, and after two rounds of in vitro they had twins. They had a third child she conceived naturally. Six months after giving birth, Amy was given a large amount of pain medicine for her headaches. She easily became addicted. After almost a year of this, she went to rehab. She stayed clean for a short time but went back to using. Wanting to get clean and feeling very unhappy, she took her kids and left her husband and close family to move to Texas with family she thought was going to help. They ruined her relationship with her immediate family. Feeling scared, she ran to a man ten years younger who had an addiction to pain meds and was very abusive and controlling. After a year of abuse, Amy and the kids came back to Illinois and lived with her parents. They were very angry at her and also are alcoholics. She also reconciled with her first husband and he moved in.

\*

AMBER PILLARS
Amber was diagnosed with
schizophrenia in 2004 at age 24

Amber Pillars is a country/small town Iowa girl. She loves to spend time with family and old friends. Amber is passionate about meeting new friends. A favorite quote of Amber's is by Will Rogers; "A stranger is just a friend I haven't met yet."

During the day, Amber can be found working with youth. She loves assisting them to grow socially, emotionally, and academically. She sees that youth need love, acceptance, guidance, and boundaries.

In Amber's free time, she continues to stretch herself in her mind, body, and spirit. She loves to read, write for fun, and is always challenging herself to learn something new. Amber enjoys watching and playing sports, especially playing volleyball. She loves going for walks and being surrounded by nature. Amber, who is in her mid-thirties, attributes her faith and trust in Jesus Christ essential to her overcoming many painful and devastating obstacles in her life.

*

DENISE PURCELL

Denise was diagnosed with depression, posttraumatic stress disorder, and dissociative identity disorder in 1995 at age 30
www.sisterdiarieswithsunshine.com.

Denise Purcell was born the oldest of seven in Syracuse, New York. She is the mother of five girls and is a talented artist, published poet, and mental health advocate dedicated to bringing about better understanding and awareness of DID and other mental illnesses.

Sunshine and Andre, another alter, are gifted artists who authored *Color Your Soul Whole*, an adult coloring book. A prolific writer, her work has been published in numerous Grief Diaries titles. Sunshine has her own YouTube series, Sister Diaries with Sunshine, to raise awareness about living with DID.

\*

ERICKA REEVE
Ericka was diagnosed with dissociative identity disorder,
posttraumatic stress disorder, obsessive-compulsive disorder,
depression, anxiety and an eating disorder in 2013 at age 26

Ericka Reeve was born in Chicago, Illinois, and has worked in the arts community her entire life. She is a writer, photographer, and model, and has published and sold her work since high school. Due to physical limitations, she is currently focused on writing and painting, though photography has always been her first love. She lives in the Midwest with her husband and their ferrets. Animals have always been a big part of her life, and that aspect of her has never left, even into adulthood.

Ericka has found amazing support through the online mental health community, and is now actively working to end the stigma surrounding mental health. DID is widely misunderstood and that nearly cost Ericka her life several times. Her and her parts are working within the community to end this damaging stigma, and to help those like herself.

\*

LORRAINE SCOTT
Lorraine was diagnosed with non-epilepsy attack disorder
and dissociative identity disorder in 2016 at age 48

Lorraine Scott was born and raised in Telford, Shropshire. As a child, she suffered from seizures which developed into non-epilepsy attack disorder by age forty-five, fully diagnosed in 2016 at age forty-eight. With all the trauma that she encountered from age five to date, she was diagnosed with dissociative identity disorder at age forty-eight. She also has degenerative disc disease and lives with three damaged discs in her spine, which is debilitating

Lorraine married in her early twenties and had three healthy children, and now has three grandchildren. She divorced in 1997, after eight years of marriage, and strived as a single mom who was devoted to her children. She married for the second time in 2015, which ended within six months.

Lorraine worked very hard and is very multi-skilled and all who know her think of her as a very strong, loving, caring, helpful, inspiring woman for whom nothing is ever too hard and is always there for others.

Lorraine is very ambitious, she enjoys sewing and crafts, health permitting, and studying and writing. She was a great dancer, and good at decorating, and DIY too.

*

CARRIE WORTHINGTON
Carrie was diagnosed with depression,
anxiety, and trichotillomania in 2000 at age 41
carrie@carrieworthington.com | www.carrieworthington.com

Carrie Worthington was born and raised in the Chicagoland area. She married at age twenty-one and moved to San Diego. In 1988, she met her second husband, and they moved back to the Chicagoland area to raise her children. She supported her family financially and her husband became a stay-at-home dad. Carrie continued to grow in her career and it gave her the ability to stay the breadwinner of the family.

Carrie's husband was diagnosed bipolar, and her son was diagnosed with bipolar and ADHD at ten. There was not a lot of support in general, and her journey into the mental illness world began. The stigma of mental illness was enormous, and resources and programs rare. She and her husband worked together to deal with the illnesses and to get through each day. This is when she started her advocacy of the mentally ill. The first mental illness she was diagnosed with was depression. She became involved with NAMI and she helped grow the NAMI Will-Grundy chapter. Her husband of twenty-two years suddenly passed away in 2011. The years following were some of the hardest she had to endure.

FROM LYNDA CHELDELIN FELL

# THANK YOU

I am deeply indebted to the writers of *Real Life Diaries: Living with Mental Illness*. It requires tremendous courage to bare such vulnerability about a topic so misunderstood. The individual dedication to seeing this book project to the end is a legacy to be proud of. I'm especially grateful to coauthor Carrie Worthington, a tireless advocate whom I admire immensely for her hard work to raise awareness and education about living with mental illness. With very little nonclinical information available, it is my sincere hope that readers who share the same path will find compassion and hope, family and friends will gain better understanding, and professionals will appreciate the candid insight.

Helen Keller once said, "Walking with a friend in the dark is better than walking alone in the light." By sharing our struggles, we learn that we aren't truly alone as we travel our journey, for there are others ahead of us, behind us, and right beside us. That is what this book is all about.

*Lynda Cheldelin Fell*

Shared joy is doubled joy;
shared sorrow is half a sorrow.
SWEDISH PROVERB

*

# LYNDA CHELDELIN FELL

Considered a pioneer in the field of inspirational hope in the aftermath of hardship and loss, Lynda Cheldelin Fell has a passion for storytelling and producing groundbreaking projects that create a legacy of help, healing, and hope.

She is an international bestselling author and creator of the award-winning book series Grief Diaries and Real Life Diaries. Her repertoire of interviews include Dr. Martin Luther King's daughter, Trayvon Martin's mother, sisters of the late Nicole Brown Simpson, Pastor Todd Burpo of Heaven Is For Real, CNN commentator Dr. Ken Druck, and other societal newsmakers on finding healing and hope in the aftermath of life's harshest challenges.

Lynda's own story began in 2007, when she had an alarming dream about her young teenage daughter, Aly. In the dream, Aly was a backseat passenger in a car that veered off the road and landed in a lake. Aly sank with the car, leaving behind an open book floating face down on the water. Two years later, Lynda's dream became reality when her daughter was killed as a backseat passenger in a car accident while coming home from a swim meet. Overcome with grief, Lynda's forty-six-year-old husband suffered a major stroke that left him with severe disabilities, changing the family dynamics once again.

The following year, Lynda was invited to share her remarkable story about finding hope after loss, and she accepted. That cathartic experience inspired her to create groundbreaking projects spanning national events, radio, film and books to help others who share the same journey feel less alone. Now a passionate curator of stories, Lynda is dedicated to helping ordinary people share their own extraordinary journeys that touch the hearts of both reader and writer.

lynda@lyndafell.com | www.lyndafell.com

Lynda Cheldelin Fell

## ALYBLUE MEDIA TITLES

Real Life Diaries: Living with Mental Illness
Real Life Diaries: Living with Endometriosis
Real Life Diaries: Living with Rheumatic Disease
Real Life Diaries: Living with a Brain Injury
Real Life Diaries: Through the Eyes of DID
Real Life Diaries: Through the Eyes of an Eating Disorder
Grief Diaries: Surviving Loss of a Spouse
Grief Diaries: Surviving Loss of a Child
Grief Diaries: Surviving Loss of a Sibling
Grief Diaries: Surviving Loss of a Parent
Grief Diaries: Surviving Loss of an Infant
Grief Diaries: Surviving Loss of a Loved One
Grief Diaries: Surviving Loss by Suicide
Grief Diaries: Surviving Loss of Health
Grief Diaries: How to Help the Newly Bereaved
Grief Diaries: Loss by Impaired Driving
Grief Diaries: Loss by Homicide
Grief Diaries: Loss of a Pregnancy
Grief Diaries: Hello from Heaven
Grief Diaries: Grieving for the Living
Grief Diaries: Shattered
Grief Diaries: Project Cold Case
Grief Diaries: Poetry & Prose and More
Grief Diaries: Through the Eyes of Men
Grief Diaries: Will We Survive?
Grief Diaries: Hit by Impaired Driver
Grammy Visits From Heaven
Grandpa Visits From Heaven
Faith, Grief & Pass the Chocolate Pudding
Heaven Talks to Children
God's Gift of Love: After Death Communication
Color My Soul Whole
Grief Reiki

Humanity's legacy of stories and storytelling
is the most precious we have.

DORIS LESSING

\*

LIVING WITH MENTAL ILLNESS

To share your story, visit
www.griefdiaries.com
www.RealLifeDiaries.com

PUBLISHED BY ALYBLUE MEDIA
*Inside every human is a story worth sharing.*
www.AlyBlueMedia.com

www.ingramcontent.com/pod-product-compliance
Lightning Source LLC
Chambersburg PA
CBHW031142020426
42333CB00013B/482